URBANISM

A.D. Architectural Design Profile

URBANISM
GUEST-EDITED BY DAVID GOSLING & BARRY MAITLAND

CONTENTS

Editor: Dr. Andreas Papadakis

First published in Great Britain in 1984 by Architectural Design
AD Publications Ltd, 7 Holland Street, London W8

Copyright © AD Publications Ltd *All rights reserved*
The entire contents of this publication are copyright and cannot be reproduced in
any manner whatsoever without written permission from the publishers

AD Profile 51 is published as part of Architectural Design Volume 54 1/2-1984

Distributed in the United States of America by St Martin's Press,
175 Fifth Avenue, New York NY 10010

ISBN 0-85670-843-7 (UK)

ISBN 0-312-83485-3 (USA)

Front cover O M Ungers, Matthaikirch Plaza, Kulturforum project, Berlin, 1983.

Back cover Rob Krier, project for Breitenfurt Centre, Vienna, 1983.

Page 1 Richard Rogers & Partner, proposal for the banks of the River Arno, 1983.

Frontispiece F. Green, project for the Kaisariani district of Athens, 1983.

Printed in Great Britain by E G Bond Ltd, London

Barry Maitland
THE USES OF HISTORY

1 Rob Krier, Breitenfurt Centre, Vienna, 1983.

Whereas Concepts of Urban Design[1] *is an attempt to excavate the successive layers of ideas which have made up post-war urbanism tracing past positions and suggesting possible future directions, this Profile offers a review of projects on the drawing board at a single moment in time. The moment is significant only in so far as some ten years or so have now passed since the crisis in modern architecture, and the divisions between architecture and planning began to direct attention to urbanism as an important and probably crucial source of authority for appropriate building solutions. These projects therefore offer an opportunity to review that hope.*

The need for an authoritative basis for design – for what Miguel Angel Roca here calls 'models of order which must be exemplary and of feasible repetition' – arose out of the belief that the Modern Movement's insistence on the programme as the source of design integrity could no longer be sustained. For if the internal logic of the problem could not provide sufficient reason for action, some other generator must be found, and where better to look than to the context in which such action should occur. Several strategies by which a contextual authority might be established were suggested, but none more forcefully than that put forward by the Rationalists, and argued by Anthony Vidler in his essay 'The Third Typology' which accompanied the 1978 publication of *Rational Architecture*.[2] Vidler proposed that whereas first nature, and then the machine, had provided legitimising models for architectural design in the past, so now the city offered such a source. 'The city is considered

as a whole, its past and present revealed in its physical structure. It is in itself and of itself a new typology.'[3] This typology sanctioned some design solutions and denied others according to whether they corresponded to, and reinforced, its characteristic typological conditions – essentially the street, the square and the quarter.

Now as Vidler acknowledged, this proposition was, in terms of the modernist position, 'indeed radical'. Despite some reassuring similarity of terminology, and particularly of the use of the word 'type', a dramatic shift of authority was envisaged. For type was no longer to be the Corbusian product of function and economy 'based on a problem which has been well "stated"'[4] but rather the outcome of history. The substitution of the past for the programme as the ultimate source of generic conditions and test of legitimate solutions could hardly be more radical.

Not that the programme was altogether denied. 'This does not, of course, necessarily mean that architecture in this sense no longer performs any function, no longer satisfied any need beyond the whim of an "art for art's sake" designer, but simply that the principal conditions for the invention of object and environments do not necessarily have to include a unitary statement of fit between form and use'.[5] Thus the modernist connection between subject and object was politely uncoupled.

Many architects have experienced an 'inversion' in recent years, in being called upon to design appropriate functions to accommodate a given form, rather than the reverse, and which has given credence to the uncoupling which Vidler proposed. And the message of *Rational Architecture*, with its common themes and

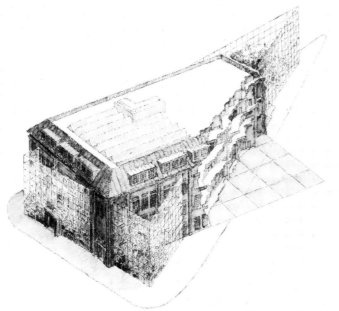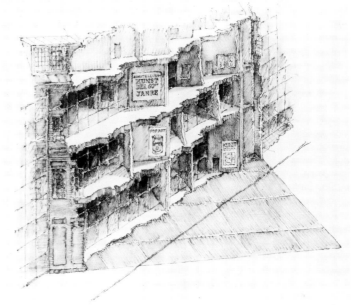

2,3 SITE, The Frankfurt Museum of Modern Art, 1983.

disciplined forms of presentation, was that we need not be afraid of such an outcome, for the Third Typology would provide an entirely adequate model 'to legitimise the production of architecture'.[6]

Now to claim this for the historical city begged the questions 'which city?' and 'which history?', and, although indicating a preference for the eighteenth-century city in Europe, Vidler refused to specify 'any polemically defined set of historical precedents.'[7] The cross-section of projects illustrated here offers an interesting commentary on the strategy, for on the one hand they almost all acknowledge history as a generator of the design, while on the other they largely ignore the particular model which *Rational Architecture* seemed to imply would achieve a natural hegemony. The city in history thus provides the themes and inspiration for contemporary action, but in novel and unpredictable ways.

The project for Breitenfurt Centre by Rob Krier perhaps corresponds most closely to the notion of typological design, with its references to universal models of agora and cloister, which are not particular to the site or its locality. In this, however, it is unusual, for in the other projects it tends to be precisely the local and specific circumstances of the city which provide the generating rules. Thus, in the second Rob Krier study for housing on Breitenfurterstrasse in Vienna, the tradition of Viennese courtyard housing between the wars is evoked and, surely, the similarly extended linear plan and fortress imagery of Karl-Marx-Hof recalled. In both of Krier's schemes 'monuments and remembrances of the site's history' take the form of heroic 'sculptural figures', occupying the key points like sentries and look-outs of their respective barbicans.

Where the context possesses some very clear historical morphology, the new project may derive its authority from its respect of that fact. The scheme by Richard Rogers and Partners to create a linear park through the centre of Florence by forming riverside walks along the hitherto neglected (in pedestrian terms) River Arno, performs the function of stitching together and enhancing an established urban form. But even in those cases where the compact and immediately recognisable form of, say, the Umbrian hill-town is not available, some model may yet be inferred from the local context of sufficient power to supply the new work with credentials – if not a model of form, then perhaps one of structure, interpolated from the characteristic spatial and organisational patterns of the place. Derek Walker Associates' plan for an area of docklands in Rotterdam provides a classic example of this approach, beginning with its analytical search through the surrounding city areas for 'structural clues' and its subsequent discovery of an 'urban geometry' of considerable richness, with layers of complexity available to generate successive levels of design. It is held to emerge from the historical circumstances of the place, but also required 'to be teased out of the existing grain of the city *as if it were already there*.' If not quite invented, history is thus massaged a little, in order to yield a context of sufficient intensity and authority for the scale of the work to hand.

Layers of meaning can be teased out of the history of a place in other ways, and once architecture is regarded as essentially a representation of history, rather than of the programme, other games become possible. This is graphically illustrated in the project by SITE for the Museum of Modern Art in Frankfurt, and spelled out by James Wines in his explanation of it, that the 'conceptual layering of ideas of *about* architecture (as opposed to "designing" architecture), becomes the entire source of the museum's meaning and its integration with the surrounding community.' Which is to say that the object, having been freed of a deterministic dependence upon the subject, now itself becomes a kind of subject, generated by its own history, whether mythical or real. Thus a style of factory building which was exported from Germany to the United States during the nineteenth century was subsequently converted into studios in lower Manhattan, where it became the setting in which much of post-war American art (including SITE's own output) was produced, and is therefore now re-exported to Germany as a Museum of Modern Art. Further histories, relating to the surrounding city or to other aspects of German-American art and architecture, are developed with their own discrete formal vocabularies, and the building then emerges as the outcome of their collision.

This use of history, with its delight in the unexpected and ironic possibilities of the place, is far removed from the typological certainties of Rationalism, and is paralleled in a number of other projects which follow. Roca's proposals for the Chilean market area of Santiago, for example, draw together the themes of the surrounding city in a series of structures and graphic elements which similarly echo, transform and intensify them. This project develops a number of features which Roca has used in the past, and particularly in the formation of pedestrian areas in Córdoba including the projection of 'shadows' of the frontages of important buildings onto the street paving pattern below, and the use of soft landscaping to mimic the forms of building elements, which give a tangible expression to the idea of public space as street theatre.

4 Emilio Ambasz, Plaza Mayor, Salamanca, 1983.
5 Bernard Tschumi, Parc de la Villette, Paris, 1983.

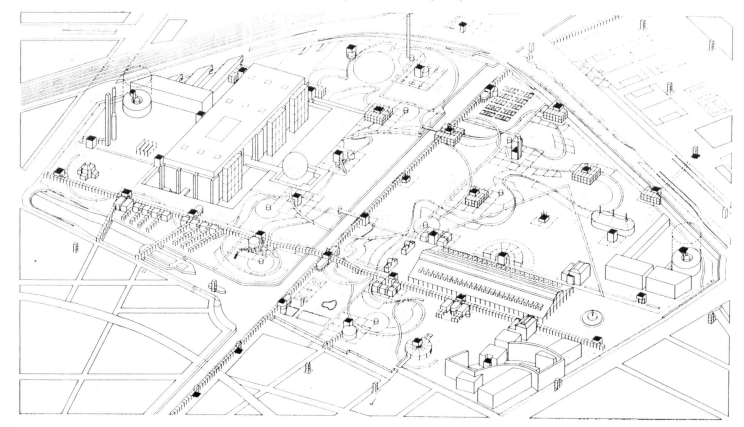

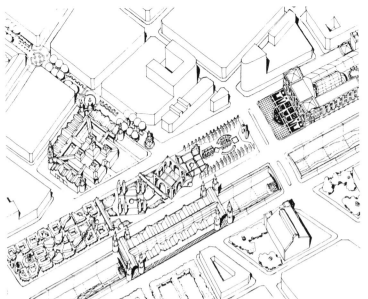

6 Miguel Angel Roca, proposal for Santiago, Chile, 1983.

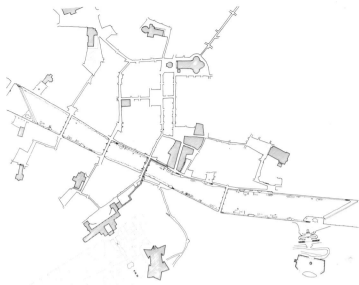

7 Richard Rogers & Partners, proposal for the banks of the Arno, 1983.

Such transformations of urban forms into unexpected images of arcadian sanctuary have long been a preoccupation of Emilio Ambasz also, and in his projects for two public spaces, Houston Center Plaza and the Plaza Mayor in Salamanca, the conventional device of planting formal rows of trees in a square becomes the opportunity to miniaturise the grid of the city, subvert its datum levels and create unexpected hidden places within it.

The poetic imagery of these projects does not deny the existence of an underlying functional programme, and indeed, in the case of the Frankfurt Museum, the historical references in the building form are as much concerned with the programme as the place. Nevertheless, the matter of how they work and are to be used seems a much less pressing determinant of their form than the explanation or challenge they provide to the city around them. There is one recent urban design study, however, in which the questions of present use and past form come into critical collision, and it is curiously appropriate that the authors of that study should be Venturi, Rauch and Scott Brown, since they offered, some ten years ago, a model an urban archetype which was precisely the opposite of that indicated in *Rational Architecture*. While it was the iconoclastic approval of commercial symbolism which attracted most attention when *Learning from Las Vegas* first appeared, in retrospect the contrast between that work and *Rational Architecture* was most significant in terms of the relationships they proposed between form and programme. For while the one extolled the 'vital mess' of the strip, in which form is entirely destroyed by the expression of frenetic activity, the other advocated 'the restoration of a critical role to public architecture',[8] in which any sign of activity is entirely suppressed by an historical typological orthodoxy. It thus seems paradoxical that the authors of *Learning from Las Vegas* should now address themselves to the problem of providing an historic town with a strategy for surviving its own commercial resuscitation. Their report, *Historic Jim Thorpe* is a carefully researched appraisal of present and potential activity in the town, and an assessment of its historic form and character. And in proposing to avoid both its petrification as an historic museum, and its destruction through unbalanced economic activity, the report is an effective refutation of both of the extreme attitudes paraphrased above. For in the end it must be doubted whether either can be sustained, whether as a satisfactory philosophy of urbanism or as a practical working method. The connection between form and programme cannot be so readily uncoupled without sterilising them both.

Yet, by a splendid historical irony, just as it seemed necessary to effect that uncoupling in order to save the city from that modernist analysis of programme which was fragmenting it, and to insist upon the discipline of street and square in spite of the functional analysis if that was what was required – at precisely that point, a strange thing occurred. For now a low-rise, block-filling, street-aligning building form was discovered (or rather rediscovered) for functional reasons which the most ardent anti-corridor-street modernist would have been obliged to acknowledge. Some of the implications of that discovery are discussed by Richard Saxon, in his recently published study of atrium buildings and their impact on urban planning.[9]

The fact that this 'new' form has extensive historical roots is particularly apposite, for to deny history absolute authority over the design process is not to deny its influence within it.

The call to order in terms of an urban typology has thus been answered in diverse and unexpected ways, sometimes passive, sometimes ironic and always inventive. Some now detect a slackening of interest in historical models of urbanism as the primary source of 'exemplary models of order'. Christopher Cross notes such a shift in student work at the RCA, for example, from typological to artistic priorities, and the invention by Bernard Tschumi of autonomous space-ordering devices for his prize-winning Parc de la Villette entry seems to reflect a similar tendency. Historical models nevertheless remain powerful sources of urbanism, and, when supportive of patterns of use, difficult to deny.

Notes
1 Gosling, David and Maitland, Barry, *Concepts of Urban Design*, Academy Editions, London/St Martin's Press, New York, 1984.
2 *Rational Architecture*, Archives d'Architecture, Brussels 1978.
3 *Ibid*, page 31.
4 Le Corbusier, *Towards a New Architecture*, Architectural Press, London 1927, page 122.
5 *Rational Architecture*, op. cit., page 31.
6 *Ibid*, page 28.
7 *Ibid*, page 28.
8 *Ibid*, page 28.
9 Saxon, Richard, *Atrium Buildings: Development and Design*, Architectural Press, London 1983.

Barry Maitland *was trained as an architect at the University of Cambridge and holds a Ph.D. from Sheffield University. After working and travelling in the US, Europe, the Middle East and North Africa, he returned to Britain to become one of the planning team of Runcorn New Town (1965-68) and the principal architect of the town centre of Irvine New Town (1968-73). He became a lecturer at Sheffield University in 1974 and was architect in charge of the design teaching practice in Sheffield. Subsequently he was the partner in charge of the Sheffield office of Building Design Partnership and is now Professor of Architecture at the University of Newcastle in New South Wales, Australia. He has contributed several articles to architectural magazines in the UK and US, and has co-authored two books with David Gosling.*

Michael Wilford

OFF TO THE RACES, OR GOING TO THE DOGS?

An appraisal of the London Docklands Development Corporation's Guide to Design and Development Opportunities for the Isle of Dogs *as an example of the gulf between city design theory and practice.*

Viscount Esher's 1984 Thomas Cubitt lecture at the Royal Society of Arts entitled 'Post-Urbanism' posed the question 'Can urban design be rehabilitated?' and was based on the premise that 'The loss of faith in planning in recent years is reflected in the policies of the present Government and in a worldwide failure to create or re-create the great city and to protect its hinterland.' He argued that architects need to re-establish a working relationship with planners and become involved once again with the public realm in order to fulfill their responsibilities to the community in general as well as to their particular client. Esher also recommended increased visual sensibility on the part of planners, the de-politicisation of local government and the development of strategies to liberate individual energies and re-establish pride within the community.

Architecture in the UK has been in the doldrums for a considerable time but it is now being suggested in some quarters that exciting things are beginning to happen again with interesting buildings and public spaces in construction. Such claims prompt questions as to whether regeneration of our cities is at last being undertaken with skill and confidence involving the examination and stimulating development of urban and architectural styles or if such optimism is merely wishful thinking and the reverse actually the case.

. . .

Urban design *is* Architecture and not a separate activity mediating between planning and building. It is the physical expression of society's hopes and intentions and a means of using and developing human and architectural potential, involving areas of concern which do not recognise boundaries between public and private domains. Currently architecture deals primarily with individual owners and properties and unfortunately, rarely crosses ownership boundaries. Planning is concerned with land use and public expenditure policy and rarely involves three-dimensional physical solutions. Urban design should integrate physical design with the power of policy-making to shape the large-scale public/private environment and manage its growth and change.

Urban redevelopment requires vigorous public/private communication and co-operation. The public sector should be encouraged by Central Government to provide stimulating physical design direction to protect the public interest and formulate appropriate incentives to inspire the private sector to respond with initiative and creative energy.

The participants are a complex group with rival professionals frequently camouflaging their differences and incompetence with statistics, lurid graphics and smooth patter. Public authorities are frequently perceived as being administered by uncreative and cautious bureaucrats fulfilling dogmatic political objectives. Developers are regarded as predators, without social responsibility and motivated only by financial gain. Planners are viewed as statisticians with their thick reports, written in abstract and opaque language (so often a substitute for ideas and action) breeding suspicion and contempt, rather than confidence, in the community. Architects have acquired the reputation of being the unprincipled hacks of developers or public authorities. The public often have

strong and differing opinions which are not easily articulated and expressed. A clear physical expression of the community's hopes and intentions through the medium of urban design is essential for the communication of a consensus image of the city of the future.

Post-war planning has turned cities into experiential deserts, has eliminated contrast and reduced sensation to a monotonous level. The spatial 'freedom' of the Ville Radieuse and its derivations has not produced meaningful cities. Disintegration of the street and organised public space which began between the two world wars was spurred on by rationalised building techniques and new traffic circulation requirements. It was argued that buildings should evolve from their own particular programmatic requirements and not be subservient to external pressures. The making of isolated buildings and the discontinuous in-fill of the residual space between them is still the norm. The public realm has shrunk to a ghost of its former self and the private realm has not been significantly enriched either. There is still restriction and lack of tolerance of 'foreign' influence in the modern city resulting in an increased poverty of meaning, the decline of invention and disintegration of conviction.

Colin Rowe in *Collage City* argues that the notion of the city of modern architecture as a panacea for society's psychological and physical deprivation is now seen to be as ridiculous as the idea that World War I was to be the war to end war. However, 'although the former city of deliverance is found to be increasingly inadequate, its expediency continues to guarantee its unadulterated and all devouring growth.'

Rowe also refers to two increasingly disparate standards of value apparent in the profession of architecture. On the one hand a concern with problem solving as demonstrated by the application of the computer, technology and behaviourist research (management disguised as science) and on the other, concern with the 'common good' as manifest in the reproduction, without intellectual variety, of useful and familiar things. He contends that advocacy planning and related populist strategies involving preconceptions of 'the people', substitute occasion and action for space and artefact, as well as mobility and choice for fixed meaning and imposition. 'Give them what they want' and similar proclamations conceal opposite aspirations of abstract scientific idealism and concrete populist empiricism. Notions that either science or people should build the town are neurotic and sterile whether considered individually or together. Both play their part but in themselves are not sufficient.

Townscape with its picturesque images of English villages and Mediterranean hill towns is still often put forward as an alternative response to the failure of modern architecture to deliver the promised goods. However, its tendency to appeal to the eye (pubs, striped awnings and cobblestones) and not to the mind, undermines any contribution it might make to a world of original ideas. Disney World, and the like, thrive in the vacuum of a weak public realm and a dull monotonous environment. They attempt to satisfy a strong human psychological craving for distinctive objects and place but avoid the complexities and realities of life, merely dealing with the crude and obvious, as machines for the production of euphoria. They fail to provoke the imagination and stimulate speculation.

Similarly, strategies advocated by the exponents of 'High Tech' which disregard context by destroying the established physical and social fabric, or which involve the literal reproduction of utopian models, employ blanket neutral grids, or stress methodology and systems, are now seen to be shallow and hopeless as means of producing a meaningful city.

Much of current planning and architecture is preoccupied with factual information and the demands of growth and change, in many cases as props and ends in themselves – 'we can't act until we have the facts and then we don't need to act since then the facts will automatically arrange themselves.' However facts, even if they can be generally agreed as irrefutable and bias-free, are inevitably overtaken by time – a consequence which, together with the precariousness of predictions of the future, will undermine the all-accommodating plan and render much of its initial investment and inconvenience redundant and in vain. Since the war considerable academic and professional currency has been given to the belief that the collection and analysis of such factual information (programme) will alone lead automatically to a credible synthesis – a proposition in which the future is to be an extrapolation of the present. More recently, propelled by the rationalist upsurge, the contention that the typical or precedent (paradigm) is the starting point for investigation has been gaining credence – a proposition in which both the present and future are to be an extrapolation of the past. Both doctrines commit us to mere repetition and do not allow or encourage invention and originality. Hypothesis should precede empirical investigation, working with programme and precedent to produce a hybrid of all researches.

Throughout the history of city design, the most satisfactory urban solutions have been those which, whilst recognising and fulfilling the necessary pragmatic objectives, have been inspired by ideas and philosophical ideals.

. . .

The lack of physical characteristics and detached geographical location of The Isle of Dogs (peninsula rather than true island) have induced a Cinderella image amongst its citizens particularly since the closure of the West India and Millwall Docks. This has now been transformed into a siege mentality by the fear of rampant commercial development of the barren areas of the Island.

Originally marshland and consequently bypassed by the expanding city, it eventually came into its own towards the end of the eighteenth century when Parliament initiated the West India Dock Company in order to build docks downstream from the city and thereby avoid increasing problems of navigation and congestion. Docks, basins and canals, were cut into the Island, warehouses constructed and storage wharves established. In the mid-nineteenth century the Island became laced with railways and housing was built for the workers. The tide of industrial development has now receded leaving dereliction and neglect in its wake but also a unique legacy of controlled water basins, several buildings of architectural interest and three vigorous communities.

Following the New Town boom in the 1960s and 1970s during which the new clean industries and their young skilled workforce were enticed away from the established cities by utopian offers of new factories, housing and schools, attention is now being focused on the plight of those left behind in the run-down inner city areas. Dwindling rate bases have created local government revenue deficits of cataclysmic proportions which, combined with the ensuing social deprivation, has compelled Central Government to initiate urban renewal programmes of which the designation of the abandoned docks in London and Liverpool as inner city 'New Towns' forms a significant part.

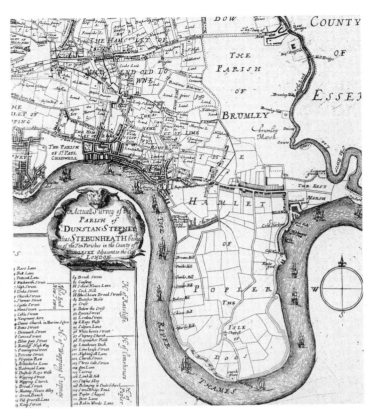

1 Isle of Dogs, 1755.

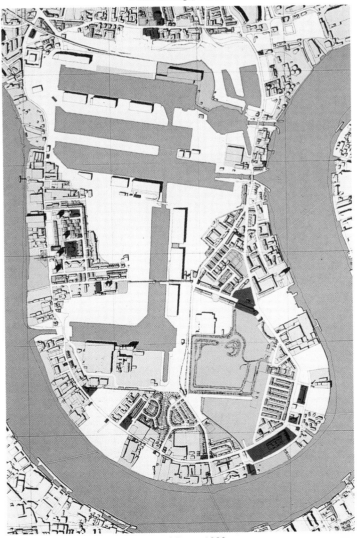

2 Isle of Dogs, 1982.

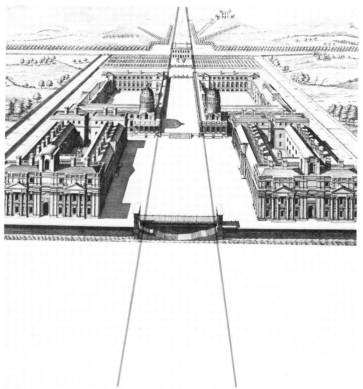

3 Greenwich axis, perspective view of the Royal Naval College and Queens House.

4 Greenwich axis, plan.

Inner city decay is not a twentieth-century phenomenon. Established European cities have often regenerated themselves in previous centuries and sustained properly integrated surges of growth, propelled by social and market forces, but always guided by an understanding of and respect for the ancient structure of the city and its monuments. Current decay is characterised by a distinct lack of market pressure for regeneration. It is still more convenient and attractive to move to virgin locations either in the New Towns or on the motorway networks. Access for employees, receipt of raw materials and delivery of finished products is easier and the quality of life alleged to be superior – everybody's dream of a house with garden front and back can be fulfilled.

The Government through its agencies has to attract industry and people back to the cities. To do this it must stress the positive characteristics of urban (as distinct from sub urban or sub rural) living supported by imaginative proposals for social and physical regeneration of the areas in question. It is therefore deeply into the business of selling, with its attendant techniques of market research, advertising and loss-leaders. An extensive media campaign (in competition with the New Towns, Development Areas and Enterprise Zones) proclaims the inducements available and the advantages of moving to Docklands – 'no development land tax and no rates payable until 1992'.

The London Dockland Development Corporation's inheritance in respect of the Isle of Dogs is rich and varied: thirteen thousand people in three communities with virtually all the dwellings and open spaces publicly owned, 5 kilometres of Thames River frontage, 53 hectares of enclosed water in the West India, Millwall, Blackwall and Poplar Docks, three conservation areas, and the majority of vacant, derelict and non-operational land vested in the Corporation. The road and public transport systems are acknowledged to be in need of restructuring and revitalisation.

A wonderful opportunity, but has the Corporation risen to the challenge?

Various planning studies, consultation reports and redevelopment proposals have been initiated since the mid 1970s by the Borough of Tower Hamlets and the Docklands Development Team (established by the Greater London Council). These contain extensive economic, land use, and transport proposals but minimal consideration of either urban design or the third dimensional component of the development possibilities. The London Dockland Development Corporation became a reality (rather than a shadow) in July 1981 with the Isle of Dogs included in the Development Area. Responsibility for the control of development was transferred from the Borough of Tower Hamlets to the Corporation, whose remit was to 'provide a speedy and efficient planning service in order to encourage development and establish confidence in the area', the inference being that the Boroughs and Greater London Council had not been expeditious and were responsible for the lack of tangible physical response.

The Corporation was established on the assumption that it would concentrate its efforts on implementation rather than plan making – leaving this task with the Borough – and would base its work on the development plans prepared prior to its inception. Its development strategies are based on 'its corporate approach to each area, acting as marketing tools to secure maximum private investment and in turn provide guidance to prospective developers on the environmental qualities sought.' This sequence is significant.

The *Guide to Design and Development Opportunities* for the Isle of Dogs published by the Corporation in November 1982 is the area development strategy which they believe responds to the particular demands of the Enterprise Zone and the Corporation's extensive land holdings on the Island. The strategy differs in a number of respects from the Borough of Tower Hamlet's draft local plan. Not surprisingly, therefore, the Corporation is at odds with the Borough and does not have the trust and respect of the community who resent Central Government imposition of the Corporation over their elected local representatives.

The *Guide's* stated aim is both 'to provide a guide to the existing character of the Isle of Dogs and to demonstrate the area's full potential for regeneration in accordance with the highest possible standards of design.' It is also claimed that 'the study will enable the Corporation to respond flexibly to individual development initiatives within the context of a strong social and visual framework.' However, the nature of the document is unclear. It is referred to as a 'guide' in its title but as a 'study' in its preface. In listing the design team, reference is made to a comprehensive 'urban design study' and specifically to Gordon Cullen's appointments as 'urban designer.'

Does the document achieve the stated aims?

The Visual Appraisal in the study identifies the community 'crust' forming the river edge of the Island, the wall enclosing the docks and the 'Greenwich axis' connecting (by design or fortuitous accident) All Saints Church in Blackheath with Hawksmoor's St Anne's in Limehouse, through the Royal Naval College and Queens House. Although the visual significance of the axis diminishes as it penetrates the Island, it is recognised as a counterpoint to the orthogonal arrangement of the enclosed water areas with potential influence on the structuring of new development. Views towards the City and Greenwich from the dock basins, mudchute and Island Gardens are plotted and attention drawn to the vast scale of the enclosed water now apparent after many of the warehouses previously enclosing the docks have been demolished.

The industrial development currently encircling the Island and the raised flood wall restrict views of the Thames to lock entrances and short stretches of public promenade. The only satisfactory relationship between river and public open space is at Island Gardens, which are raised to the level of the flood wall. Connections between the loop road and the 'mainland' of Poplar are restricted and emphasise the isolated nature of the Island. Existing communities have identifiable centres but only one – the largest, Manchester Road – possesses a sense of place through its streetscape and buildings.

The section on Townscape Structure explores and explains the visual framework of the Island in minute detail, extracting and recording every possible asset from what might be easily perceived as a desert of dereliction. An analogy is drawn between the disposition of communities along the loop road and beads on a string (nodes and links) and the asymmetry noted between the riverside wharves on one side and the high wall enclosing the docks on the other. A strengthening of the string of beads concept is recommended to enhance the urban structure of the loop road, by clarifying the street corridors and centres of community. The individual identity of the Island is noted despite its close proximity to the city and four main characteristics are identified –community, water, Greenwich and the mudchute (an artificial hill formed from dock dredgings).

Analogies to 'magnetic fields' and reference to a 'visitor exploration axis' in the *Guide* are difficult to relate to the present reality and to comprehend as tangible bases for regenerating the Island. Why are the community 'circuit' and visitors 'route' considered to be separate rather than overlapping characteristics of the plan? The visual structure plan prompted by these concepts lacks conviction and strength of image.

The sequence of views supporting the Conceptual Diagram are careful studies of the existing situation and, in respect of the 'crust', make interesting and sensitive proposals for capitalising, with modest means, on the potential of the existing fabric. However, gateways, enclosing walls, additional views, adjustments to road alignments, and other landscaping elements aimed at building a coherent network of identifiable spaces are likely to be considered

5 *Guide* perspective view along Millwall Dock.

6 *Guide* sketches of 'Millwall arcade'.

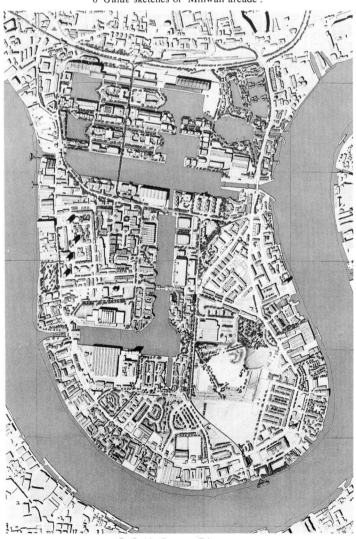
7 *Guide* Concept Diagram.

by residential and commercial developers, given the option, to be an extraneous expense. Even if one accepts Gordon Cullen's contention that it would be self-defeating to produce a rigid design brief for the whole area, the question continually arises as to how the proposals or alternative versions of comparable quality and presence are going to be achieved. The form, location and scale of buildings necessary to give credence to the Conceptual Diagram must be set out by the Corporation (however open in their detail and material characteristics) in order that spaces which depend upon several different developments can be coherently realised by the private sector. Many of the proposals also relate to the public realm and will have to be executed in whole or in part by the Corporation.

The absence of urban ideas for the centre of the Island (the whole of the dock area as distinct from the water's edge) and the lack of implementation proposals are likely to make the Conceptual Diagram more tenuous and turn the image conveyed by the sketches into a cruel mirage. Arcades and perspective views along aligned buildings in a common relationship to the water depend upon a coordinated approach to development for their realisation.

The Concept Diagram makes no proposals for a small representative area to be left untouched as a ruin and memory of the docks in their prime.

The most disturbing and frustrating section of the Guide is the Development Framework. It is concerned with the public realm but does not respond to the opportunities presented by the Island. The emphasis is on provision of serviced development sites in a 'strong and attractive framework' and the Corporation's committment to a flexible attitude to development proposals. The decision to retain the enclosed water is unequivocal but recommendations regarding development in the dock basins are unclear. The importance of a strong landscaped framework for development is noted but generalised references to continuity of open spaces, buffer areas, the structure and unification of spaces by tree planting and entreaties about the scale and species of trees to be employed, all emphasise the weakness of the 'guide' approach to redevelopment. The proposals for public open spaces – parks and gardens – are vague and fail to explore the unique potential of the existing water and mudchute.

Due to the absence referred to earlier of strong and overriding urban ideas, the Design Studies convey the impression of a struggle to cover the space available with development in mix and texture similar to that which exists in the 'crust' and to camouflage or tame the vigour of the docks. The scale and extent of the enclosed water appears to have been intimidating and is consequently treated with caution and reserve. The studies compromise and confuse rather than exploit and enhance the Island's unique characteristics.

The conceptual studies prepared by David Gosling represent approaches based on clearer urban structures and stronger relationships between the public and private realms than those indicated by the Conceptual Diagram. His options advocate the strong and coherent public realm necessary to organise the inevitable variety of architectural form and quality entailed in the Enterprise Zone concept. In option 3, for example, the All Saints/ St Anne's axis together with vistas, topographical relationships and the new movement systems are suggested as the bases of a suitably vigorous framework within which individual developments can be accommodated. It is unfortunate that these studies were not presented in the Guide as alternative strategies alongside the Conceptual Diagram rather than consigned to the Appendix and represented merely as preliminary work.

The concluding paragraphs of the Guide are full of meaningless jargon and platitudes. We know from earlier statements that the central concept is one of flexibility but how can a 'succession of self-contained development moves each point to a new synthesis of the whole Island' and how will the Island 'acquire greater clarity

and richness by allowing the various identities to become the essence of its evolution through a subtle network of dialogues and relationships'?

Did the Corporation really want to make and publish an urban design plan but was prevented by its remit from doing so (implementer rather than planner – guide rather than plan)? Was the Corporation reluctant to risk deterring potential clients by establishing a positive (too constrained) framework for development or did Gordon Cullen's opinion that it would be self-defeating to produce a rigid design brief coincide with a prior decision by the Corporation not to produce an overall design? The various descriptions applied to the Guide betray confusion and lack of purpose within the Corporation and are likely to circumscribe any influence the document may have. Hard-nosed developers are unlikely to respect a 'guide' or pay attention to a 'study' unless compelled to do so.

Is the Isle of Dogs really likely to become 'one of Britain's most stimulating and productive environments for living, working and recreation'?

The evidence to date is not encouraging. Regrettably developments completed or in construction and projects published replicate the incoherent and diluted characteristics of suburbia. It appears that land owned by the Development Corporation is being parcelled, cleared, serviced and sold to developers with little regard to the form of development proposed. New housing is predominantly of the 'Noddy' variety with the familiar cosmetic devices (eg stepped plan relationships, pitched pantiled roofs and porches) thought to give a commercially safe form and appearance. A mixture of dwelling types and sizes is required to provide appropriate urban forms. Likewise, commercial development completed or in construction suggests either free-standing 'pavilion' buildings situated cheek to jowl with each other and separated only by parking and security fences, or the repetition of the monotonous light industrial buildings seen on the fringes of so many of our cities. Both types are unrelated to the new streets and water. An exception in visual terms is Indescon Court, but even this group contemplates its own navel, disregarding its neighbours and the street serving it. The Asda supermarket is a visual and experiential disaster. Its location has no relationship with either the established or proposed communities and the building itself is interiorised, with entrance related to parking rather than street.

A recent Docklands advertisement boasts of the decision by the Daily Telegraph to move its printing operation from the City to the Island, but siting a large automated printing plant adjacent to the Millwall Dock is inconsistent with the Guide's stated objective of exploiting the visual potential of the water and is unlikely to generate any significant public activity on the quay. A positive planning attitude would steer such development to one of the landlocked sites.

What the Isle of Dogs needs (and deserves, after all the studies made and reports published) is a positive and exciting urban design presented in a manner which will give an identifiable image to the Island and re-establish its importance in Central London. Such a design would not preclude rapid assessment of planning applications if this is essential to the real – rather than commercial – success of the Enterprise Zone, but could stimulate the interest and imagination of newcomers and provide some assurance to the existing communities that regeneration is not going to swamp them. It would also act as a guarantee to public and private investors that the area really will be developed to the highest design standards.

. . .

Aldo Rossi in The Architecture of the City reminds us that man has always built with aesthetic intention which, together with the creation of better surroundings, comprises the two permanent characteristics of Architecture. He states that Architecture, attesting to the tastes and attitudes of generations, is the fixed stage for human events and invests man's inhabited and constructed realm with value. Rossi believes that expropriation, demolition and rapid changes in use as a result of speculation and obsolescence are clear signs of urban dynamics and that monuments, as signs of the collective, constitute fixed points in this dynamic. Imagination and memory are, in his opinion, primary characteristics of urban artefacts. Rossi also states that the city cannot be reduced to a single basic idea. It is comprised of many distinctive parts with numerous and varied processes of formation.

Lewis Mumford in *The Culture of Cities* states that the city is a conscious work of art. 'Mind takes form in the city, and in turn, urban forms condition the mind, for space, no less than time, is artfully organised in cities. The city is both a physical utility for collective living and a symbol of those collective purposes and unanimities that arise under such favouring circumstances. With language itself, it remains man's greatest work of art.'

The city is an icon, signifying attitudes to historical process and social change, raising questions of symbolic purpose and function. Its design should contain both order and disorder, the simple and complex, permanent reference and random happening, innovation and tradition together with the retrospective and prophetic gesture. History tells us who we are, what we have achieved and provides a rich resource of types and precedents from which to study, learn and apply.

A clear hierarchy of spaces is essential, ranging from places of public assembly through to private living. Rather than being allowed to go everywhere it is far more satisfying to be presented with the restraint and stimulation of a clearly constructed ground plane. Buildings and spaces should co-exist in a condition of alerted equilibrium. Authenticity of architectural experience is what distinguishes place and the exaggeration of that experience necessary to mark a place as special demands clarity in the diagram of the city.

It is vital that we rediscover texture, colour, noise and other experiences which create an atmosphere full of deviations and surprises. The history of urban design has demonstrated that successful urban spaces are always related to a sequence of private space. There should be a mutual exchange between the public realm and private or institutional spaces. The city is activated by the relationship between both aspects as witnessed in, say, St Mark's Square in Venice or a London Georgian Square – on one side social standing, representing the group and on the other, institutional or domestic territory in all its various expressions.

A sense of purpose and conviction should direct the endeavours. Dependence on the capacities of non-regulated capitalism as fairy godmother has been demonstrated time and again to be a deluding myth and cowardly evasion on the part of those charged with the task of designing our cities. Ironically, the making of architecture in an era which supposedly eschews design for the sake of profit becomes even more crucial in a depressed market which increases the buyer's range of choice because of lack of demand. Architecture is a means by which differentiation can be made.

. . .

The Corporation should either have a policy which it sincerely believes in and administers with vigour or abandon all pretence. A policy which is infinitely flexible is a travesty and the Guide is unlikely to have little use or significance beyond a public relations exercise. Unfortunately the Corporation does not appear to have the ideas and determination necessary to exercise its power for the maximum benefit of the new enlarged community.

It would be especially ironic if the sacrifice of urban design standards thought necessary to ensure the commercial success of

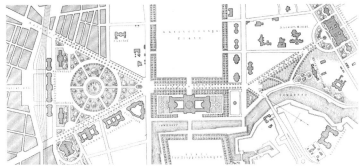

8 Plan for the centre of Tokyo.

9 Plan of the centre of Turin.

10 Plan of Regent Street and Regent's Park.

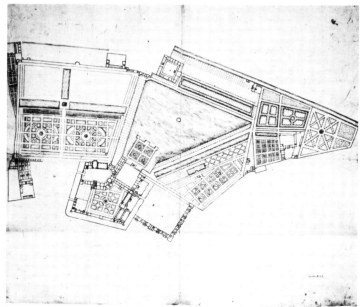

11 Plan of palace, Fontainbleau, c 1600.

12 Plan of gardens, Fontainbleau, eighteenth century.

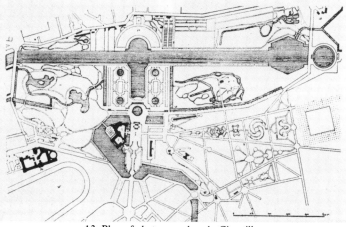

13 Plan of chateau and park, Chantilly.

the Enterprise Zones is not subsequently justified by employment generation. A recent report concludes that the cost of establishing employment in Enterprise Zones has been high and the type of firm attracted has not been as expected. By May 1983, 8000 jobs had been created at a total cost to the Exchequer of £133 million.

The apparent contradiction of preparing an urban design for an area of which a substantial part has been established as an Enterprise Zone, could have been resolved by making the public realm the key visual element in the character of the Island's development as suggested in Gosling's early Conceptual Studies. The elements which comprise the public realm constitute major items of the Development Corporation's investment and are therefore within its direct control. Buildings could have the role of backdrop and the particularities of their design would be of secondary concern to that of their relationship with the street and to each other.

The dock basins constitute unique planning and landscape opportunities for which architects (and their patrons) of previous generations were prepared to move heaven and a lot of earth to create. The possibility of using the relationship between the orthogonal geometry of the basins and the diagonal All Saints/St Anne's axis as a basis for restructuring the Island, although acknowledged in the Visual Appraisal section of the *Guide*, has been either overlooked or dismissed in the Conceptual Diagram. If the potential had been more fully appreciated and the challenge taken up, the new infrastructure could have been more legibly and memorably configured, focusing on bold new public spaces for assembly and entertainment related to the docks in a manner similar to that in which cities established on river edge or ocean front formally address the water. The new 'centre' could have been connected to sub-centres in the existing communities and to the 'mainland' by a hierarchy of avenues, squares, streets and courts.

Appropriate densities and mix of development must be achieved to sustain the envisaged level of urban activity with day and night vitality. Retail, commercial and entertainment functions should be concentrated along streets and pedestrian routes with offices and housing at first floor level and above. Rigid zoning must be avoided.

Greater clarity is required between open space and urban fabric by means of defined edges (as in the London Parks) for the transition from one to the other to register and for the contrasting experiences of community and park to be appreciated. St George's Gardens provides a good example of the urban space required on the Island. Regeneration together with the space and large unused buildings available also provides an ideal opportunity for generous provision of indoor and outdoor sports facilities. The 'crust' should be connected at numerous locations through the dock wall to the core of the Island by means of streets and pedestrian routes. The proposals in the *Guide* are likely to perpetuate the present separation between core and crust – a characteristic no longer relevant and one which must be eroded if the different areas of the Island are to be integrated.

Connections with Poplar need to be enhanced following construction of the relief road across the northern edge of the Island in order to provide discernible gateways and to reduce the sense of separation. The people of Poplar and Borough of Tower Hamlets should feel free to use and enjoy the enhanced amenities of the Island.

In the case of the Isle of Dogs, the new enthusiasm noted at the beginning of this essay is prompted by the once-in-a-lifetime opportunities of redevelopment but, regrettably, any new confidence is unlikely to be justified by the quality of urban design generated by the *Guide* and the Corporation's laissez-faire implementation process. By pitching its design objectives so low, the Corporation has denied itself the opportunity of achieving anything but a mediocre visual and experiential environment. The Concept Diagram is simplistic, recognising neither aspect, prospect nor topography in a positive manner and does not exhibit an ideal base strong enough to withstand the inevitable warping and distortion of the process of implementation. It does not express either an exemplary image or mood of confidence and credibility. It is a highly innocent diagram and appears to have been based on caution, modesty, and the least possible imposition – an approach which Rowe has termed 'the theory of maximum non-intervention'.

A comparison can be made between turf accounting and the Corporation's role in the regeneration of the Island. The professional life of a bookmaker is one of calculated risk-taking. In response to the strength of betting he continually adjusts his odds to levels sufficiently attractive to the punters but which also minimise his exposure. The Corporation's reaction to unsatisfactory or inadequate development proposals cannot be as flexible and immediate. The odds have to be fixed at the outset and should therefore have been as 'short' as possible to allow subsequent 'lengthening' only if particular circumstances would benefit from it. Nash as architect/planner/developer and selling agent, risked his reputation and livelihood to realise Regent Street, Regent's Park and other notable achievements. Where are his late twentieth-century equivalents?

It will be claimed by those responsible for the redevelopment of the Isle of Dogs that these criticisms of the *Guide* ignore the realities of the situation. However, it is always possible to marshal a list of reasons why something could or should not be done but there can be no excuses. We are not the slaves of circumstance. In recent years several studies have been published on the essential characteristics of cities and strategies proposed for their regeneration. Ideas and entrepreneurial skills are available with a wealth of first class design talent and experience available in the UK for the Government and its agencies to draw upon. Promises are being betrayed and opportunities squandered but we must still hope that the Corporation's enabling powers will be combined with appropriate design skills to produce examples of real presence and urbanity, not only for this and subsequent generations to revere but as contributions to the art of city design.

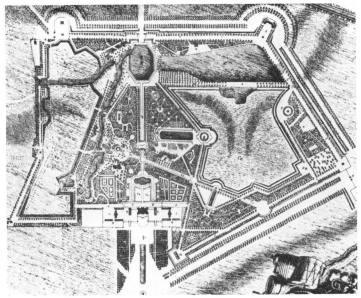

14 Bridgeman plan of Stowe gardens.

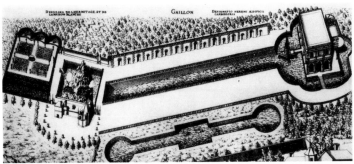

15 Aerial view of chateau of Gaillon.

Sources and acknowledgments
Rowe, Colin and Koetter, Fred *Collage City* , MIT Press, Cambridge, Mass., and London, 1978; Rossi, Aldo *The Architecture of the City*, Opposition Books, MIT Press, Cambridge, Mass., 1982; Mumford, Lewis *The Culture of Cities*, Harcourt Brace & Co., New York, 1938; *Isle of Dogs. A Guide to Design and Development Opportunities*, London Docklands Development Corporation, London, 1982; Bacon, Edmund *Design of Cities*, Thames and Hudson Ltd., London, 1967 revised edition 1974; Stübben, Joseph *Der Stadtebau*, Friedr. Vieweg & Sohn, Braunschweig and Wiesbaden, 1980; Benevolo, Leonardo *Corso di Disegno*, Editori Laterza, Roma-Bari, 1976; Marie, Alfred *Jardins Français*, V. Freal, Paris, 1955; MacDougall, Elizabeth D. ed. *The French Formal Garden*, Dunbarton Oaks Trustees for Harvard University, Washington D.C., 1973; The Cornell Journal of Architecture No 2, 1983.

Michael Wilford studied at the Northern Polytechnic School of Architecture and started but did not finish a course at the Regent Street Polytechnic Planning School in London. He has travelled extensively throughout Europe, North America, Africa, Middle and Far East and has acted as lecturer, critic, and external examiner at Schools of Architecture in the UK, USA, and Canada. He is currently a Visiting Professor at Rice University, Houston, Texas and Graham Willis Professor at Sheffield University. He was a member of the Royal Institute of British Architects Education and Professional Development Committee (1979-1981). Formally associate and now partner with James Stirling, he has worked on projects extensively published and discussed worldwide: these include the Faculty of Engineering, Leicester University; the Faculty of History, Cambridge University; Dorman Long Headquarters, Middlesbrough; Runcorn New Town Housing; Olivetti Headquarters, Milton Keynes; School of Architecture, Rice University; Department of Chemistry, Columbia University; and the Performing Arts Center, Cornell University.

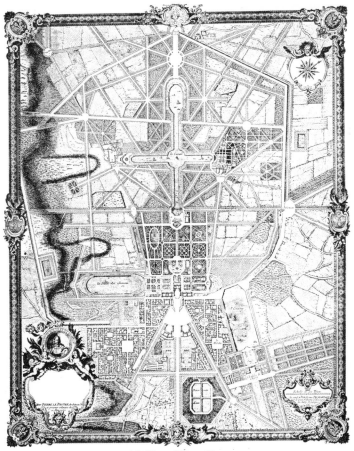

16 Plan of Versailles.

David Gosling
DEFINITIONS OF URBAN DESIGN

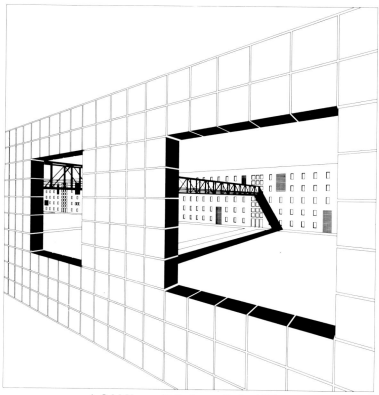

1 O M Ungers, Kulturforum, Berlin, 1983.

Concepts of Urban Design[1] is an attempt to provide a review of urban design theories which have appeared over the last few decades, but it was not the intention of the authors in the preparation of this work to take any particularly polemical stance. During the preparation of this work it became apparent that an analysis of the forces which controlled the form of cities, whether they were economic, social or political forces, was necessary to arrive at some general definitions of those forms. Hence the city as process was seen as the result of an emphasis on economics, the city as a technical device as a result of engineering considerations, the city as an expression of social order as a series of attempts at social solutions, the city as a resolution of design problems in terms of professional solutions and the city as coherent experience in terms of formal solutions. It is this last definition which leads inevitably to considerations of some of the present projects assembled under the loose title of 'Urbanism'.

In the assessment of future directions, analyses and predictions were made in the context of the radical reappraisal of urban design theory which has occurred during the last decade, particularly with the argument of the Rationalists for a Third Typology and their central concern with the morphology of the city. If the case studies in *Concepts of Urban Design* illustrate an enormous variety of attitudes and preoccupations of urban designers, they could not, by their very nature, give any clear indication of future directions. The case studies were never intended to be a representative sample because the mere range of examples precluded this.

The Modern Movement adopted the functionalist view of the city in which urban design implied a definition of the city as a homogenous product in formal terms. Javier Cenicacelaya Marijuan would describe this attitude as related to a variable politico-cultural system, that is, a descriptive view of the city divided by functions and classified by dominant activities. This is the opposite of attitudes dependent on a particular politico-cultural system, whether a Marxist concept of the city or a Utopian concept.[2]

The functionalist theory would blame the chaos of the city on a lack of clarity in the subdivision of the city by functions and such an indiscriminate mixture can only favour chaos. Le Corbusier, in referring to the construction of new blocks in the centre of Paris which replaced the obsolete structures, said 'Nobody interferes. On the site of the old city, which was so destructive to life, a new city is rising, which will be even more deadly to life, in that it is creating real centres of congestion without any modification of the street.'[3] This comment could be taken as a curious contradiction by Le Corbusier where his own urban design proposals did in fact ignore the morphology of nineteenth-century Paris. Since the functionalists regard the city and its growth as divided by functions,[4] standards are used for analytical measure and as criteria for future proposals with the different functions researched within the city. The city then achieves the second typology, that of the industrial order symbolised by the machine. The city becomes a machine for living (*machine à habiter*). The city is divided into its constituent parts, for living, working, shopping, recreation, transportation and the city itself becomes part of a larger structure within the territory which might include university cities or industrial cities. A late twentieth-century example of this early twentieth-century dream is the aberration of central Brasília, originally planned and constructed within a democracy but curiously reflecting the aspirations of the military regime which followed.[5]

We argued in 'Future Directions'[6] that the *mono-technic* city which was implied by the Modern Movement is functionally inappropriate. The *bi-technic* city comprises two distinct technological zones. The Nazi 'Blut und Boden' philosophy was based upon this in which the monumental and technically advanced places of work and public ritual envisaged for the city centre by Albert Speer or Ernst Sagebiel contrasted with the vernacular hearth and home associations of the residential 'Schaffendes Volk' estates. But this interpretation was by no means confined to societies of the far right. An examination of the Third Phase[7] New Towns in Britain showed a similar dichotomy between town centre uses and residential areas, albeit within the more benign influence of a Welfare State. If the town centres reflected an attempt to incorporate the highest degree of technological innovation into the concept of a 'town which is enclosed', the housing areas were intended to reflect the aspirations of the inhabitants who hoped for privacy in an arcadian and traditional setting.

At a more mundane level, the actuality of cities in the industrial or post-war world are also divided into the technological zones of the central business district on the one hand and on the other suburban 'houses with clapboard siding and a high-pitched roof and shingles and gaslight-style front porch lamps and mailboxes set up on top of lengths of stiffened chain that seemed to defy gravity...'[8] as any viewer of the current American television soap operas will confirm.

Such a *bi-technic* division was described by us as a 'crude simplification of the ancient association of the most advanced and expensive technology with the most powerful building types which themselves tend to congregate in the areas of highest land value. This suggests a picture of the city as a spectrum of technologies, hierarchically ordered, from the most exotic house of God, King, State, or Business Corporation, to the most modest structure for the domestic pet.[9]

The idealisation of a mono-technic city can be challenged by the reality of a multi-technic one. Not even Brasília can be classified as an example of newly formed, precisely contemporary construction at a specific instant in time. The city undergoes a continual process of modification because of the huge areas of steadily obsolescing material. We may recognise this as a matter of fact, but we may also welcome it as a fundamental characteristic of a valid urban design approach, in which the city is seen as an unpredictable compound of technologies.

In his introductory essay, Barry Maitland discusses Anthony Vidler's notion of a Third Typology where the city itself was to be the source of legitimate architectural design: history, rather than Corbusian function or economy, would have thus been the source of urban types. Nonetheless, there has been a declining interest in historical models as sole exemplars of urban order. The following selection of projects committed to the topic of 'Urbanism' was not arbitrary, but neither was it a deliberate attempt to include just projects devoted to the 'Third Typology'.[10] Rather, it was an attempt to invite a diverse, even disparate, group of internationally acknowledged urban designers to display what are mostly hitherto unpublished projects in order to discover whether there is indeed a shift away from the Third Typology towards new directions.

It may be useful to reiterate some principles associated with the Third Typology. If the historicism of such writers as Lewis Mumford or Chueca-Goitia[11] is based upon a generalist approach to cultural historical periods, that of the writers concerned with

urban morphology and building typologies is specialist in approach and more directly related to design theory. Architecture is considered here as the primary element in the construction of the city, through history, with a sense of permanence, locus, monument and memory.[12]

In history, there are separate building typologies accorded to the different cultural periods and locations. These typologies determine the form of the city, within a total infrastructure, including transportation networks, and including the open spaces (the public realm of places and squares) and the containers (the private realm of buildings). Thus:

1 Typology is concerned with the construction types in a particular urban situation.
2 Morphology is the formal expression of the construction types taken individually or as a whole.[13]
3 Open space is the container, the 'rest of the urban form' or the public realm. It is this public realm which provides the semiology, the system of orientation for the inhabitants of the city. They perceive the city through the public realm as a coherent entity or they do not if the public realm is imprecise.

In attempting, then, to define new directions through the projects illustrated here, it is apparent that a majority acknowledge history as the generator but, as Barry Maitland points out, 'largely ignore the particular model which *Rational Architecture* seemed to imply would achieve a natural hegemony'. It is inevitable that the projects of Rob Krier are closely related to typological design and urban morphology. But other projects evade such straightforward categorisation. Derek Walker's Rotterdam project, for instance, whilst acknowledging the contextualism of the city, neither adheres to the functionalist programme of his buildings at Milton Keynes nor is especially concerned with building typologies in the manner described by the Rationalists.

Concepts of Urban Design set out categories in one of the concluding chapters concerned with future directions of urban design. Thus, Minoru Takeyama's Row House projects (1974-78) and the squatter settlement of Christiana in Copenhagen were seen as *Urban Design as Political Statement* because each infers an appropriate social order, one in a highly regulated society, the second a model of tolerant anarchism.

Urban Design as Technique suggests that the work of the late Donald Appleyard at the University of California, Berkeley or the MIT Architecture Machine Group provides methods of analysing the city structure but not necessarily of providing solutions. Bernard Tschumi's Manhattan Transcripts (1978) provide a more rhetorical commentary on the search for new analytical methods for the city.

Urban Design as Mediation looks at the essentially neutral techniques of such theorists as N J Habraken whose *Supports* was more in the nature of a manifesto than finite design proposals, although the subsequent work, *Variations: the Systematic Design of Supports*,[14] does elaborate on design possibilities. Gaming simulation systems are also discussed in this category.

Urban Design as Private Display refers to the work of Roger Walker in New Zealand whose buildings celebrate the idea of advertisement and the more literal but spectacular designs of the American design group SITE, with the incorporation of apparent building failure as an experiment in advertising technique for supermarket design. Reference, too, is made to the seminal study *Learning from Las Vegas* by Venturi, Scott Brown, Izenour and Yale architectural students.

In *Urban Design as Public Presence* Emilio Ambasz's project in Michigan (1975) is used to describe the evocation of civic presence through the construction of key public buildings in a manner familiar to nineteenth-century European architects.

Urban Design as Theatre is an extension of this idea from a

2,3 Lucien Kroll, Les Vignes Blanches, 1976–.

collection of individual buildings to an extended pattern of actions. Whether it is an example of Cullen's attempts to create a village in the Highlands of Scotland (1974) or Portoghesi's proposal for uniting dispersed residents in an Italian rural community (1981), the urban form suggests a strategy of sequentially experienced events.

Urban Design as the Guardianship of Urban Standards, the final category, relates much more closely to the theories of the Rationalists and the Third Typology. Such a strategy depends upon the establishment of stable formal categories, drawn from the analysis of existing cities and the use of these as the agreed basis of future action. The most comprehensive view occurs in Rob Krier's book *Urban Space*[15] or his brother Leon's compilation of the morphology of quarters.[16] But the Third Typology has been undermined by forces additional to the preferences of the Modern Movement, and these must be recognised as a change in direction. The project by O M Ungers, Rem Koolhaas and others at the Sommer Akademie of Berlin in 1977, which sought to define an effective urban design strategy for that city, rejected the notion that the historic quarters of the city must be preserved at all costs and pointed to the depopulation of Berlin which undermined the basis of a return to historic forms.

If the new Rationalist description of the city proves to be too restrictive and too insensitive to forces within it, the categorisation of theoretical directions must be reappraised. It might have been simple to allocate the projects presented here within the categories listed above, but an attempt to do so inevitably fails.

In examining future directions in urban design we asked the questions: What is the nature of the design problem posed by urban design? What are the aims and limitations of the urban designer's activity? On the one hand we have Rob Krier's adoption of the severe and highly controlled vocabulary of the new Rationalism and on the other hand we have Venturi's model of the Strip and his preference for 'vital mess'.[17] Furthermore, if Venturi's study of Las Vegas was classified originally as Urban Design as Private Display, that classification would not apply to the study of the town, Jim Thorpe, in Pennsylvania. It is possible that some of these original classifications do apply and perhaps one of the most interesting applications of Urban Design as Political Statement

would apply to Lucien Kroll's interesting account of proposals for Le Quartier des Vignes Blanches. Kroll's celebrated design for the University of Louvain might have originally been considered in this category too but was regarded as Urban Design as Mediation in the sense that Kroll attempted to open up the design process to users and place the designer in the role of orchestrator. Even SITE's project for the Museum of Modern Art in Frankfurt by James Wines and Alison Sky might be categorised as their earlier work under the heading of Urban Design as Private Display but would more appropriately come under some entirely new category of architectural inversion where the form or site is given and design focuses on the incorporation of new functions and use.

A. Urban Design as Mediation
As the only remaining category from *Concepts of Urban Design* which is truly appropriate here, Lucien Kroll's statement concerning his project for Les Vignes Blanches at Cergy-Pontoise clearly shows his continued preoccupation with the involvement of the citizen in the urban design process. In an interesting book published recently,[18] Kroll shows from his project for the University of Louvain (Quartier des Facultés Médicales à Woluwé) how an immense degree of individual choice was achieved through a rationalisation of component design and suggests in other projects as yet unbuilt how his social objectives may be achieved through the banal techniques of component cataloguing and computer-aided design. His essay published below refers to the 1976 competition for town houses in the new town of Cergy-Pontoise, near Paris. He suggests, both in his book *Composants*, as well as this present case, that banality in architecture or urban design has long been a pejorative term[19]. He describes meetings with the inhabitants of Cergy-Pontoise to explain to them how they intended to work and also to listen to their ideas. The problem, symptomatic of all new town construction, was of meeting the needs and aspirations of the present inhabitants as well as those of the newcomers. In *Composants* he says that the monotonous repetition of building in the nineteenth-century was not the result of industry or the metric system which were the cause but impotence and an endemic blindness. Kroll says that his project at Cergy-Pontoise is 'not a glorious realisation: just banal;

4 SITE, Paz Building, Brooklyn, 1983.

5 Emilio Ambasz, Houston Center Plaza, 1983.

that it should not be published like a piece of art but like a testimony'. Nevertheless, his 'banality' has all the intricacy and complexity displayed at the University of Louvain as, presumably, a direct response to the inhabitants. Such a view is a polarisation in the framework of urban morphology and building typology.

B. Urban Design as Revitalisation
As a direct contrast to the ebullient celebration of Las Vegas and the Strip, the project for Jim Thorpe, a nineteenth-century mining town in the mountains of Pennsylvania, by Venturi, Rauch and Scott Brown, is a profound study into the salvation of an historic town. On the one hand there is the objective of preventing fossilisation as a tourist attraction, and on the other that of avoiding its destruction through normal economic and commercial forces. Based upon comprehensive and thorough research, the report[20] contains a description of the town which is powerfully evocative.

If historical models remain powerful sources of urbanism in general, this essay in revitalisation of an historic settlement does not rely upon the reproduction of urban morphology but its retention and controlled extension.

C. Urban Design as Inversion
SITE's proposal to convert an eighty-year-old YMCA building in Brooklyn, New York into a multi-use commercial space shows a continuation of SITE's powerful use of imagery. The designers suggest that this imagery should reflect the general spirit of the community with its conditions of contrast. Themes such as old/new, decay/rebirth, worldly/religious and closed/expansive are seen to be visually evident in the neighbourhood. In contrast to the entertaining 'building failure' structures of their earlier work, SITE have produced an impressive, if somewhat sombre, emergence of a new building from the ruins of the old and reflect, in a way, Peter Cook's more recent interests in the architecture of decay.

SITE's other project for the Frankfurt Museum of Modern Art is perhaps more interesting for its use of interpenetrating structures, a device seen elsewhere in the work of Ungers and others. Whilst in a sense it is an historicist study using a German factory prototype, it contradicts the view of the urban morphologists in actually distorting or at least disturbing the urban fabric upon which it is placed.

Miguel Angel Roca's scheme for the market in Pratt Square, Santiago cannot truly be classified as inversion in urban design but rather as urban intervention, but it nevertheless conceives of both the maintenance of the present fish market activity 'by means of collective memory and the presence of the people' and also the recovery of the present structure and its restoration with its new use as a meeting centre, replacing the confusion of small food and handicraft stores to the periphery. As well as the recycling of the internal space for new community use, Roca proposes the demolition of the other accretions and reconstruction using light, elegant metallic structures as a way of exalting the old building.

D. Urban Design as Iconography
Emilio Ambasz's project for the square in Salamanca in Spain is a deliberate reversal of the conventional role of a central city space. By planting a 'forest' in the square, Ambasz creates a great natural canopy so that as well as the square acting as a garden in the city, it also acts as the city in the garden. Houston Center Plaza is a more sophisticated essay on the same theme. This garden with its powerful imagery reverses the normal role of the city centre with its underground theatre, restaurants, and exhibition areas. If Place Ville Marie and Place Bonaventure created the underground city for Montreal in the late 1960s, Ambasz's Houston project creates a dialogue between the outside and inside, a vision of Arcadia, which was not achieved in the Canadian project.

E. Urban Design as Internal Space
Rob Krier, in the recently published issue of *Architectural Design*[21] sets out an interesting theory relating to the design of interior space ('Explanations Relating to the Typology of Interior Spaces'). Whilst his concern is clearly to do with the design of buildings, his diagrams of the development of interior space (page 19) are clearly to do with the city. He says: 'The diagram shows in the horizontal the geometric ground plan forms: square, triangle, circle and amorphous figure; and in the vertical the possibilities of transformation of these basic elements by way of addition, penetration, buckling, breaking, accentuation of perspective, or

effect of depth and distortion.' Obviously the historical precedents are many, like Borromini's or Michelangelo's use of the accentuation of perspective in the creation of urban space in Baroque Rome. But Krier's concept of overlapping space and space within a space has a curious link with a peculiarly late twentieth-century building type, often with no apparent historical links except in name.

F. Urban Design as Spatial Matrix
Derek Walker, whose most publicised designs are probably the puritanical grid buildings of Milton Keynes, has more recently shown some changes in design direction, especially in his detailed design for the Wonderworld Theme Park for Corby.[22] Walker's project for the Docklands area of Rotterdam was amongst a limited number of design invitations which included Aldo Rossi, Richard Meier, Josef Kleihues and O M Ungers. If the complexity of the radial form of central Amsterdam has some basic coherence, the street plans of Rotterdam reveal an exceedingly intricate and directionless pattern, making orientation for the stranger an impossible task.

The area is one of derelict industry and half-abandoned dock workings but with the inhabitants of different ethnic groups. The regeneration of this area called for the construction of 9,000 houses. Walker points out the essential difference between planning a new town in virgin territory whether in Britain or the Middle East and creating an urban structure within a major existing city. The existing grain of the city, complex as it is, was seen as the originator of a new route structure. Like the Amsterdam Canals, the Rotterdam drainage channels have a type of grid formulation which, with cross routes forming other linear elements, create a pattern of nodes or 'foci of heightened activity'. Walker argues that the broken characteristics of the area suggested that the route structure which would form the functional and spatial matrix for the proposals required complementary characteristics. It should be, he says, 'an extension of the existing structural frame of the city, a tensile force providing spatial continuity in scattered locations, a satisfactory interpretation of the city's formal texture and a basis for the design of a series of urban spaces giving the area a sense of unity and identity.'

Now it is interesting that this successful attempt to reinterpret the grain of the city emphasises a concern expressed by other urban design theorists whose ideologies might be seen to be quite different. Kevin Lynch's studies of some twenty years previously made much of the importance of urban grain and now this work of the empiricists, as Geoffrey Broadbent terms Lynch, Appleyard, Cullen and their adherents, is subject to a quite different approach of a finite, highly precise urban design plan.

If the Royal College of Art students established a justifiably high reputation a few years ago in the field of urban design, it was clearly based upon theories of historical reference. Strongly influenced by both Edward Jones and Christopher Cross during the last ten years, some of the earlier projects clearly belong in a different category of urban design.

Christopher Cross acknowledges that by the end of the 1970s, due perhaps to increasingly gloomy economic conditions, both tutors and students alike became critical of working at an over-ambitious scale. The Metal Exchange Project of 1980 under the direction of Christopher Cross examined ways of building to support the tight medieval network of the traditional city and there are parallels with Derek Walker's Rotterdam project. Cross says that '. . . it sought to demonstrate that careful infill at small scale could complement the old system without compromising artistic integrity – urban dentistry.' Other examples indicated the distinction between monument and fabric as in the investigation of the network of terrace houses in Inner London, and more especially in the transitional area between the inner city and the suburban fringe as in the 1981 Urban Villas Project directed by Edward Jones. This project of villas as free-standing solids was contrasted with the unbuilt voids of the Paris Courts in the Hôtel Particulière Scheme of Fernando Montes.

G. Urban Design as Definition of the Public Realm
Various definitions of the public and private realms have been given in descriptions of the Third typology. Elsewhere[23] great importance has been attached to the creation of a sufficiently strong public realm in physical and visual terms as essential to the success of any urban design project. If, in that reference, the private realm is broadly classified as the design of individual buildings or groups of buildings, either for the public or for private individuals,

6 Derek Walker & Peter Barker, Docklands, Rotterdam, 1983.

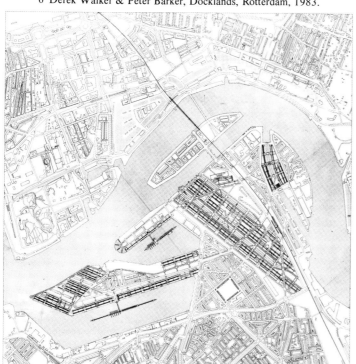

7 RCA student project for Holland Park by Graham Fairly, 1979.

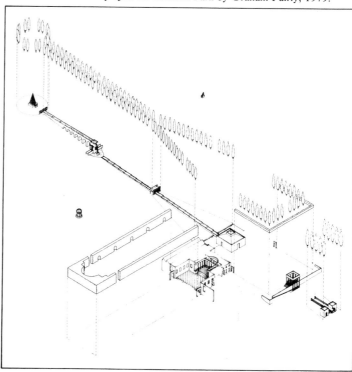

the public realm is the ordering system of the city: the squares, streets, quarters, transportation systems whether public or private and the pedestrian network.

The following examples do not necessarily have the same clear historical references as the final category of the Third Typology but they have as great an emphasis on the ordering system as the more clearly historicist schemes of the Rationalists.

O M Ungers' limited competition project of 1983 for the Berlin Kulturforum epitomises such an approach. Located in a key area of Berlin adjacent to the Hans Scharoun complex of buildings, including the Berlin Concert Hall and Mies van der Rohe's Berlin Art Gallery as well as the as yet unbuilt Science Centre project by James Stirling, the problem of creating a coherent urban structure might appear almost unsurmountable. Yet the final outcome of Ungers' study is a masterly piece of entirely coherent urban structure.

The site occupies the entire urban space between the Askanischem Platz and the Lützowplatz and Ungers proposed a necklace of buildings along the Landwehrkanal. The axonometric drawing shows Ungers' entire three dimensional concept aimed at uniting all the disparate parts of this area. In the centre of the district, the Matthaikirchplatz, the church (Stuhlkirche) and the parish community centre form an angle-building relating to each other diagonally opposite corners. This plaza and its angle-building, in an inversion, reiterate the geometry of Mies van der Rohe's National Gallery on the opposite side of the street whilst the expansion to the Gallery itself to the west reflects the volume of the original building but instead of being set within a plaza introduces four small courtyards within the building.

To the east, Ungers has created a tower building standing on a platform similar, if not identical, to the podium construction of the National Gallery. Ungers defines the building with five viewing 'plateaux' every eight floors permitting an overview of the city at different heights. The top of the tower is a glass-enclosed city museum with the tower divided into five functional sections. The existing hotel is seen as the integral foundation of the complex.

The old Potsdamer Strasse remains as an historical fragment linking the two sections of the urban core with the new Potsdamer Strasse determined by two further angle-buildings, the inner zone

of each enclosing public areas. To the east of the tower and forming the boundary of the area is a development of city houses as square blocks each within a separate plaza, again reflecting an inversion with the inner courts of the National Gallery extension.

Ungers elaborates on these main elements and emphasises the character created by each. The plaza for the Matthaikirch must, he says, remain free and deliberately pure in its geometrical form. The community centre develops from the open space of the plaza outward towards the street, forming a complete wall. The plaza symbolises 'meditation, compilation, separation and completion.' The community building which contains the monks' cells at second floor level is linked to the Matthaikirch by an underground walkway. The housing areas on Potsdamer Strasse develop as a pair of angle-buildings each with a gallery facing the street and the other side facing a self-contained inner park, whereas the rental housing to the east on the site of the former Potsdam railway station is developed in a uniform network distribution. Each block is four-storeyed containing either four dwellings or two maisonettes, each approached from an outward facing staircase and gardens freely shaped in front of each entrance.

Bernard Tschumi's well-publicised winning design for La Villette competition makes an equal if quite different impact on the public realm to that of Ungers' Berlin project.[24] At two separate levels the project reflects, perhaps accidentally, design antecedents from elsewhere and certainly from outside Europe. Significantly one of the competition assessors was the talented Brazilian landscape architect, Roberto Burle-Marx. Alex Wall comments upon Burle-Marx's exotic tropical designs which complemented modern urban architecture in Brazil. Indeed, the modern baroque forms of Affonso Reidy, Oscar Niemeyer and others necessarily required the dazzling colours and curvilinear forms of Burle-Marx's gardens. Thus the dramatic forms envisioned by Tschumi for the urban park of La Villette do not summarise the grand formal tradition of French landscape architecture and in no way can be considered historicist. Another analogy occurs in the curvilinear forms of the late twentieth-century fun fair or theme park. The interlocking geometries of highly complex gravity rides, when seen on engineering drawings, have such a startling resemblance to Tschumi's plans, the casual observer may be forgiven for thinking

8,9 O M Ungers, Kulturforum, Berlin, 1983.

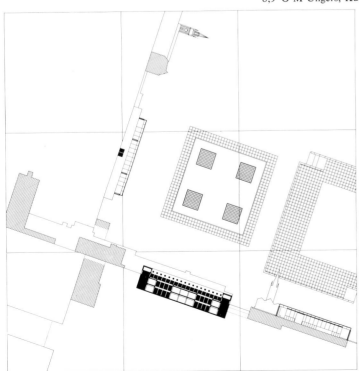

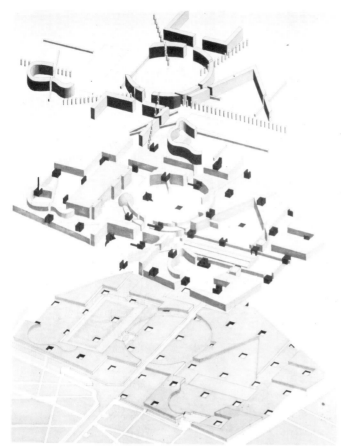

10 Bernard Tschumi, Parc de la Villette, Paris, 1983.

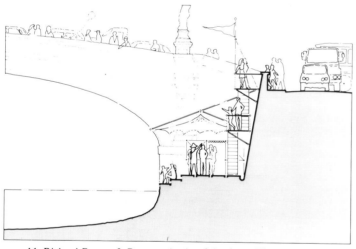

11 Richard Rogers & Partners, banks of the Arno, Florence, 1983.

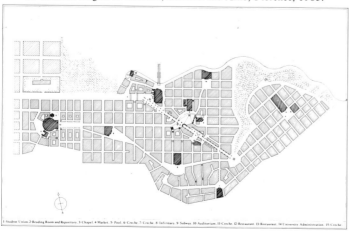

12 PCL student project for the Kaisariani Quarter of Athens by F Green, 1983.

at first sight that this is indeed an urban fun-fair similar to parts of Copenhagen's Tivoli Gardens.

Bernard Tschumi has more profound objectives than this, however. He says that the park forms *part of the vision of the city*. 'The competition for the Park of La Villette is the first in recent architectural history to set forth a new programme – that of the "Urban Park" proposing that the juxtaposition and combination of a variety of activities will encourage new attitudes and perspectives. This programme represents an important breakthrough. The '70s witnessed a period of renewed interest in the formal constitution of the city, its typologies and its morphologies. While developing analyses focused on the history of the city, this attention was largely devoid of programmatic justification. No analysis addressed the issue of activities that were to occur in the city. Nor did any properly address the fact that the organisation of functions and events was as much an architectural concern as the elaboration of forms and styles. The Park of La Villette, in contrast, represents an open-air cultural centre, encouraging an integrated programmatic policy related both to the city's needs and its limitation.'[25] The proposal is based on a theoretical argument treating the city as a whole rather than as an accumulation of zones and pockets.

It is slightly ironic, therefore, that a guru of high technology design, Richard Rogers, was commissioned to carry out an intensely historical study for Florence, which was to create a linear park through the centre of the city by developing riverside walks along the banks of the Arno. The scheme is a skilful knitting together of the public structure where building design is of secondary importance in a scheme of routes and links.

H. Urban Design as the Third Typology
(Urban Morphology)

Christopher Cross, in his description of the activities at the Royal College of Art, mentions that the 1977 Barcelona Project typically summarises preoccupations of that time. He says 'the frustration and impotence of architects when faced with the full development of the modern city (for which of course they have hardly any responsibility) and a lingering megalomania from the last throes of the Modern Movement provoked a reappraisal of historic precedents.'

Leon Krier was highly influential in the London schools of architecture, including the Royal College of Art, and emphasised the importance of the urban block as a key social and physical element in maintaining cohesive city structure prior to the mid-nineteenth century. Hence, as Cross points out, 'In contrast to the prevailing circumstances in which armies of specialists might surround themselves with data and labour for years to organise the typical chaos of a modern city it seemed there should be a return to the use of traditional systems and paradigms. With a rediscovered understanding of these systems it might be quickly possible to propose new cities or, more believably, interventions within old cities.'

So the interest in urban morphology as urban design procedure has come to dominate both theory and urban design practice in the last decade and the last examples discussed here include the work of some of the most important theorists, including Rob Krier and Maurice Culot.

The work of students under the direction of Demetri Porphyrios clearly demonstrates their adherence to historical precedent. The urban interventionist project in the Ayia Kaisariani Quarter in Athens is a typical example of such work with an intricate manipulation of a sequence of public spaces along a diagonal axis through the existing rectilinear grid of the quarter.

Maurice Culot's project for 'The Battle for Corner Properties in Brussels' is a profound and important study of urban disintegration. Carried out as a survey with four subsequent projects at the

Archives d'Architecture Moderne, Brussels, in 1983, it is based upon the belief that the physical state of any urban situation can be assessed by the state of preservation of corner properties. If, in terms of urban morphology, the street is considered the prime ordering element, then the street intersections are equally critical.

Culot says that until the 1930s the angled plot was considered as choice terrain for a wide variety of different developments and even at a base economic level of the nineteenth-century British industrial city the local shops were established at corner intersections because these were seen to be the nodal points of the community. After the Second World War, corners were neglected and either decayed or were destroyed. Culot believes that this threatens the fundamental cohesion of the traditional urban structure and 'visually amplifies the city's state of aesthetic degradation.' The study was carried out to establish a political priority for the renovation and reconstruction of corner properties.

By no means confined to the European city of Brussels, such destruction of the urban fabric is a valid problem of urban decay in most major cities of the world yet probably overlooked and misunderstood as to the symptoms of decay and its cure.

Barry Maitland suggests that Rob Krier's Breitenfurt Centre corresponds most closely to the notion of typological design with clear references to the historical models of agora and cloister. Krier says that the settlement is amorphous and fragmented in the manner of an American suburb and suggests the introduction of a designed agora or market place to give order and focus. Ideally, a church would have provided this central focus but, since this did not exist, Krier suggests the embellishment of an existing recreation hall with a symbolic tower-like structure. A semi-circular building for a small town hall closes the square formed on the other three sides by the agora, with the light well of this building stressing its internal monumentality. The primary and junior schools which form the flanking buildings have a cloister system opening out onto the central space. Krier suggests that the architecture's continuity offers the suburb or village a symbolic place of political and religious assembly.

The second project by Rob Krier is for housing on the Breitenfurter Strasse in Vienna and has obvious links and analogies with pre-World War II public housing projects in Vienna, with their great central courtyards and arched accessways beneath the blocks. In this project, the site is long and narrow in an apparently decaying part of Vienna bounded by abandoned waterways. But the use of image buildings, such as the round tower flanked by ramps, tends to introduce a much needed light-heartedness for a fairly extensive public housing scheme. His use of fountains and monumental figures are equally significant in this sequence of events.

Projects by the Sicilian architect, Bruno Minardi, offer a similar interest in spatial relationships based upon historical paradigms. The plan for New Calatafimi was to provide new housing for 1,000 inhabitants after damage by earthquake. The architectural elements have closer links with the designs of Aldo Rossi than Rob Krier, and he uses towers and rotundas in a similar manner to the former architect. The project, Minardi says, is intended to give the area an urban appearance with the plan based upon three elementary observations of the complete confirmation of the existing street layout, the confirmation of the connectional extra-urban axis and the choice of an orographical element as an organisational feature. The thoroughfare is marked during the day by a tall row of palms and at night by a 'forest of multi-coloured neon signs'. The entrance is spanned by a restaurant (similar to motorway restaurants) forming a huge coloured gateway.

A second project by Minardi has even more curiously interesting architectural forms. This is an urban design for development of the canal port of Mazara del Vallo founded upon

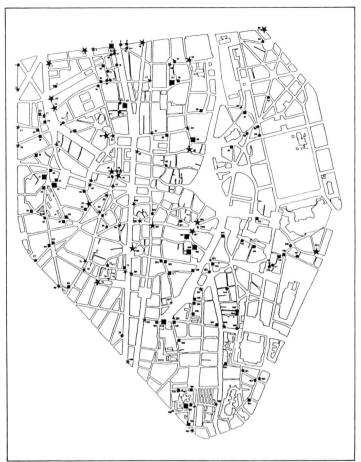

13 Archives d'Architecture Moderne, dilapidated corner sites in Brussels, 1983.

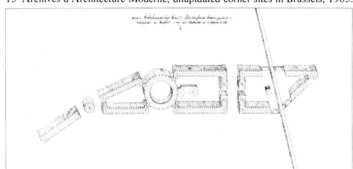

14 Rob Krier, Breitenfurterstrasse, Vienna, 1983.

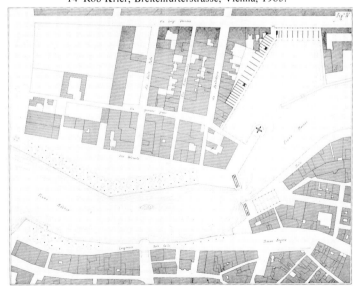

15 Bruno Minardi, Mazaro del Vallo, Sicily, 1983.

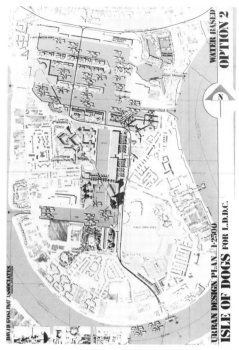
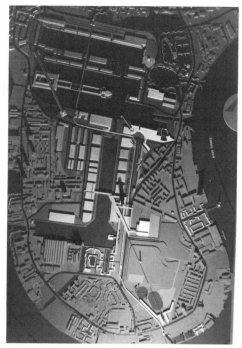
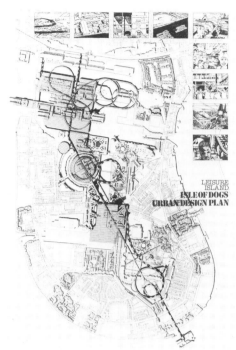

16-18 David Gosling Associates, Isle of Dogs study: alternative option 2 (of 4), model and study for the Royal Academy exhibition.

the ancient town of Mazara which has served variously as Phoenician port, Roman castrum and Byzantine town. By combining isolated elements and built spaces within which repetitive building groups can be inserted, Minardi attempts symbolically to reflect the images of dock machinery in his architecture, which includes a dramatic lighthouse constructed of a metal trellis.

A New Definition of Urban Design

Michael Wilford, in his essay, provides a more comprehensive overview of urban design than has hitherto been established by many other urban theorists. The decline of public confidence in public authorities, developers, planners and architects has been well rehearsed many times. As Wilford says, 'A clear physical expression of the community hopes and intentions through the medium of urban design is essential for the communication of a consensus image of the city of the future'. He condemns the disintegration of the street and organised public space, but suggests that whilst this public realm has all but disappeared, the private realm is not significantly better. Perhaps Wilford is correct in saying that picturesque images of English villages and Mediterranean hill towns are no sort of answer, nor for that matter the high technology images which destroy the physical and social fabric and the reproduction of utopian models. But perhaps he is not as correct when he supports Colin Rowe's rejection of advocacy planning and related populist strategies. Surely an attempt to discover popular needs, so elegantly described in Lucien Kroll's account of his design activities at Cergy-Pontoise, is also a way of regenerating and distinguishing between the public and private realm.

In a perceptive criticism of urban design proposals for the Isle of Dogs in London Docklands, carried out by the London Docklands Development Corporation, Michael Wilford remarks that the corporation was established on the assumption that it would concentrate its efforts on implementation rather than plan-making, leaving this task with the Borough (of Tower Hamlets), and would base its work on development plans prepared prior to its inception. In an article 'Cities'[26] it was pointed out that the Borough of Tower Hamlets had produced three relevant documents for the Isle of Dogs of which the most important was the Consultative report, 'Isle of Dogs: A Plan for the 1980s', published in 1981. In the four optional studies prepared by David Gosling Associates in

opposition to the rest of the report, cognisance was taken of Tower Hamlets' own land use proposals, particularly in option 1. These four optional studies, which were consigned to an appendix and described as 'initial conceptual studies' when in fact they were produced concurrently with the Development Framework Plan, were an attempt to represent an amalgam between the public and private realm. The view taken was that the urban design study should not be a series of statutory proposals but rather a prospectus to engage the interest of the existing community, local authorities and potential industrialists in promoting a rational and imaginative development[27]. Michael Wilford says these 'early conceptual studies . . . demonstrate approaches based on clearly discernible urban structures. . . it is unclear why these ideas were not incorporated into the final conceptual diagram'. This goes back to the central theory that given a strong enough design structure for the public realm, an immense variety of alternatives can be conceived in the private realm.

If the need to discover popular requirements is valid, Lucien Kroll's planning methods of Cergy-Pontoise might point the way. The achievement was considerable, for in doing this they began to unite the aspirations of the existing villagers as well as the incomers in a way which was never achieved in the consultative processes used in British New Towns. Kroll describes it thus: 'Three movements: first, the landscaping intentions for the village towards our terrain: colours, roofing, alignments (not the 'New City' style). It was the assembled villagers who spoke to the eventual inhabitants. Following this, the "real inhabitants" closed themselves up, at first in their kitchen, their living room, bedroom, finally on paper . . . . All this had been registered (for fear of our professional deafness), analysed and interpreted immediately by rough forms and general plans'. This level of involvement by present and future inhabitants of a community was probably only paralleled in this country by the work of Ralph Erskine and Vernon Gracie at Byker, Newcastle.

In *Concepts of Urban Design* we said 'The need to reaffirm the primacy of a common, social pattern of spaces in the city to which developments gave rise were no less great in those parts of the world where the massive immigration of rural populations to the city threatened its fabric in different ways. It might be argued that the priorities in a country like Brazil, for instance, should be concerned more with the solution of grave economic issues and social injustices than with the niceties of urban design, but this implies a narrow cosmetic view of the subject belied by experience of communities in the Third World. The traditional favela (shanty town) system of Brazil, or the barriadas of Peru have a coherent physical structure for all their ad hoc construction and unsanitary conditions – perhaps more importantly, a coherent social structure. Based upon principles of self-determination[28] in terms of both physical and social development, they contrast markedly with authoritarian plans for their replacement by massive inhuman multi-storey "conjuntos"'; or, as Lucien Kroll says 'The anti-establishmentarians of yesterday are the powers of tomorrow and are preparing themselves to be as annoying'.

Now Lucien Kroll's work at Cergy-Pontoise might be paralleled by earlier work in Brazil by Carlos Nelson dos Santos in the reconstruction of the Bras de Pina favela in Rio de Janeiro in 1967. Carlos Nelson dos Santos and a team of young architects rehabilitated a favela of some 4,500 inhabitants by living in the favela and interpreting the needs of each family by asking each household to prepare a plan of its housing requirements. These planners, working with a kit of parts of prefabricated timber units, attempted to provide a house as close as possible to the requirements of the individual family. Successful in visual terms in their reflection of the vernacular architecture of the original favela, they were developed from some 300 requested plan variations and translated into a typological study of thirteen different models.

Lucien Kroll extends this technique which he describes in *Composants*[29]. He proposes that the use of building techniques such as prefabrication, or kit of parts, as well as design technologies such as computer-aided design are not necessarily counter-productive in the generation of communities and give freedom of choice and self-determination to inhabitants. The indication is that such techniques might speed up a system of creative anarchy and self-determination. Perhaps the public realm could provide an absolute freedom of choice in the private realm.

NOTES

1 Gosling, David and Maitland, Barry, *Concepts of Urban Design*, Academy Editions, London/St Martin's Press, New York, 1984.

2 Marijuan J C, 'Towns in Expansion – Historicist Approach or Perceptual Approach', M.A. dissertation in urban design, Oxford Polytechnic 1978.

3 *Le Corbusier in A.C. (Documentos de Actividad Contemporanea)*, Barcelona, 1934, page 250.

4 'Such a concept of function, taken from physiology, assimilates the form of an organ, in which the functions justify the form and the variation of the functions means the change of the form. So, functionalism and organism, the two main streams that have presided over modern architecture, show the common root, the cause of their weakness and fundamental misunderstanding.' Rossi, Aldo, *L'Architettura della Citta*, Marsilio, Padova 1966.

5 The classification of cities in this way is by no means a twentieth-century phenomenon. Jacques Francois Blondel in his *Cours d'Architecture* listed the various kinds of buildings in the architect's repertory and these were classified according to the dominant function to which the building was dedicated. However, the idea of the separation of functions and later of zoning was a town planning device introduced within the last forty years or so.

6 Gosling and Maitland, *op. cit*.

7 Post-1945 British New Towns have been popularly separated into three phases of development. The new towns mainly based upon London and constructed in the 1950s included Harlow, Stevenage, Crawley and others and were based upon Scandinavian architectural prototypes and the Garden City ideal. The second phase, epitomised by Cumbernauld started in the early 1960s, introduced dramatically new planning concepts including higher housing densities and vertical pedestrian vehicular segregation. By the mid-1960s the third and final phase of new towns again departed radically from previous planning theories, including a reaction against conventional circulation systems and a separation of emphasis on different functions within the town, whether industrial, town centre or shopping uses. Runcorn, Irvine, Washington (County Durham) and later on Milton Keynes were such examples.

8 Wolfe, Tom, 'The "Me" Decade', *Harpers and Queen*, January 1977, page 48.

9 Gosling and Maitland, *op. cit*.

10 As defined by the Rationalists in *Rational Architecture*, Archives d'Architecture, Brussels 1978.

11 Mumford, L., *The Culture of Cities*, New York 1938, republished in expanded form as *The City in History*, Penguin Books, Harmondsworth 1961. Chueca-Goitia, *Introducion al Urbanismo*, Madrid 1970.

12 There are even differences between some of the main representatives of this movement, such as Rossi and Aymomino. If for Aymomino the architecture for the city is a continuous demonstration of the relationships between the parts, and constitutes a precise operation included within a spatial structure, for Aldo Rossi, in his Gallaratese project, a linear residential building is placed beside the building designed by Aymomino; the architecture does not need to have an immediate contextual relationship. For Aymomino and Rossi, even if the sense of the operation is extraordinarily convergent, the study of the constructional elements, the lack of context (*decontestualizzazione*) and reconstruction of a new meaning, the difference is in the field, in the process; dialectical, real and physical for Aymomino and pre-dialectical, a priori, conceptual and indifferent to the historical period* for Rossi. Gina Conforto, Gabrielle de Giogi, Alessandra Muntoni, Marcello Pazzaglini, *Il dibattito architettorico in Italia, 1945-1975*, Bulzoni Editore, Roma 1977.

   *Aldo Rossi displays this in his 'Citta Analoga, Tavola' in *Lotus International*, No 13, Milan 1976, page 5.

13 Morphology or urban morphology was defined by Carlo Aymomino as 'The study of built form considered from the point of view of its production in relation to the urban structure' in *La Citta di Padova*, 1970 by C. Aymomino, M. Brusatin, G. Fabri, M. Lena, P. Lovero, S. Lucianetti and A. Rossi.

14 Habraken, N J et al, *Variations: the Systematic Design of Supports*, MIT Press, Cambridge, Mass 1976.

15 Krier, Rob, *Urban Space*, Academy Editions, London/Rizzoli, New York 1979.

16 Krier, Leon, 'The Cities Within the City II: Luxembourg', in *Architectural Design*, Vol 49, No 1, 1979. Also Enrico Guidoni in *Lotus International* 19, June 1978.

17 Venturi, R, Scott Brown, D, Izenour, S, *Learning from Las Vegas*, MIT Press, Cambridge, Mass 1977, page 52.

18 Kroll, L, *Composants: faut-il industrialiser l'architecture?*, Editions Socorema, Brussels 1983.

19 'Those who treat banality pejoratively wish to impose great authoritarian schemes and to order all the details of form; they speak of great architecture when it is rather a question of expressing the power they have, and they efface many great contributions, even those that may be mature and responsible: it is diversity which is the enemy.'

20 Venturi, Rauch, Scott Brown, 'Historic Jim Thorpe: Historic Preservation and Commercial Revitalization', report to the Carbon County Planning Commission, Pennsylvania, February 1979, page 13.

21 Krier, R, 'Elements of Architecture', *Architectural Design*, 53 9/10-1983, pages 18-51.

22 'Animated Architecture', Guest-edited by Derek Walker, *Architectural Design* 52 9/10-1982.

23 Gosling, D, 'Isle of Dogs: Discrepancies in Approaches to Urban Design', in *Cities*, Vol 1 No 2, November 1983, pages 150-166.

24 Wall, A, *International Architect*, Issue 1 1983, pages 26-31.

25 Tschumi, B, 'Un Parc Urbain Pour le 21e Siècle', competition report, 1983.

26 Gosling, D, *op. cit*.

27 The point being made here was that the four options were only a preliminary sample. Hundreds of alternatives might be drawn up, all equally valid, provided that the framework of the public realm was sufficiently strong. In fact, two subsequent urban design studies were made by David Gosling Associates to prove this point. They were not commissioned by the Development Corporation but carried out as self-indulgent exercises and exhibited at the Royal Academy Summer Exhibition in 1983. A recently published scheme (Jan 1984) by Nicholas Lacey for the West India Dock on The Isle of Dogs bears a strong resemblance, though unacknowledged, to the theme of the Option 2 plan prepared by David Gosling Associates.

28 Described in Gosling, D, 'Housing Case Study in Brazil' – II Vila 31 de Marco, Belo Horizonte, *Architectural Design*, Vol 45 January 1975, pages 38-41.

29 Kroll, *op. cit*., concluding chapters.

David Gosling *studied architecture and town planning from 1951 to 1960 at Manchester University School of Architecture, Massachusetts Institute of Technology and Yale University. He practised as an architect until 1973 as deputy chief architect for Runcorn New Town (1965-68) and chief architect/planner for Irvine New Town (1968-73). Since then he has been a Professor of Architecture and later Dean of the Faculty of Architectural Studies (1977-81) at the University of Sheffield, and he has also acted as an assessor, visiting professor, adviser and external examiner to educational establishments throughout the world and as a consultant to several urban design teams, including most recently the London Docklands Corporation. A frequent contributor to leading architectural magazines and publications specialising in the problems of the third world, he is also co-author with Barry Maitland of* The Design and Planning of Retail Systems *and* Concepts of Urban Design.

Lucien Kroll
LES VIGNES BLANCHES, CERGY-PONTOISE

1 Perspective of design proposals.

No, I am not going to draw up a theoretical text on urbanism, but rather relate an actual experience and then deduce from it a few general words.

BANAL
'*Banal, banaux*: that which pertains to a public announcement; public or common kilns, mills, the people of which served a manor lord to whom they paid rent.'

Banal is thus machinery which not only everyone *may* use but *must* use. The pejorative derivation of 'banal' – 'vulgar', 'common' – is significant: from it one marks the divergence between cultural classes, between the sublime and the vulgar, between submission and cooperation, between domination and participation, etc.

Those who treat banality pejoratively wish to impose great authoritarian schemes and to order all the details of form; they speak of great architecture when it is rather a question of expressing the power they have, and they efface many great contributions, even those that may be mature and responsible: it is diversity which is the enemy.

The Competition
1976 – We were one of sixteen prize-winners in the competition 'City Dwellings' in Hautil, held by the new city of Cergy-Pontoise to the west of Paris. A district committee was already acting on the New City and persuaded it to explore the course of community participation and of evolution after construction. And the New City had authorised by statute that during the course of several years the purchasers would be able to transform and construct annexes of up to half the original surface (would they build a new shanty town?). Worried about finding architects who would respond to this, and knowing our interest and experience, the New City invited us to participate.

Visits to Cergy (how do the inhabitants of a new city live?), then staying in the house of an inhabitant, debates with other architects who wanted to do everything together . . . Then back in Brussels, too far away, we preferred to draw up our proposition after what we had seen of the site, simulating amongst ourselves the possible intentions of the inhabitants and the negotiations of the neighbourhood. Each one of us took a house, projected his personal views onto its

organisation, its dimensions, its uses; then, with simulated 'neighbours', tried to organise communal actions. All of it resulted in an image, after all rather life-like, of diversity and cooperation between objects: its very disorder exorcised predispositions that may have been too mechanical or too personal.

Slightly foreign, we happily served the project because we had received the most beautiful terrain right near the village of Vincourt: it had been refused by a powerful developer because the gradient towards the Oise River was too steep and car access seemed insufficient to him . . .

The Participants
A little too hastily we had declared: 'no inhabitant, no plan'. But in a new village inhabitants are hard to find: we asked the Town Planning Office of the New City to introduce us to families who had come for information about the possibilities of purchase or the location of the New City. They procured for us a list of about 30 eventual inhabitants. We wrote to each one of them that some architects wished to make contact with possible inhabitants in order to

2-6 Views and sketches of neighbouring villages.

avoid false steps, then we telephoned several of them to find out if they would come to a meeting. And with a big model and numerous documents about the context and possibilities, all the working stock to register their expressed wishes, we went to the rendez-vous one Saturday afternoon in September.

No Inhabitants, No Plans

And no one came. Because of the date, the time, the place, the text of the invitation, one didn't know. Deceptive reflection, each had his own. Rallying to the defence, I said to myself: 'absurd': turned around on the autoroute to see again the terrain which, to me at least, was a reality. By chance I returned to the house of a wine merchant who lived in an old farmhouse in the village of Vincourt adjacent to our terrain. In his cellar, I chose several bottles. I would return in two weeks.

— Wait, are you from nearby?

— No, I'm an architect and . . .

— Ah! I'm glad to see you, I've got a wall, I want to buck it up but everybody criticises me. Besides, we've started a small association which protects the character of the old village.

I was offended:

— In the face of 2,500 projected lodgings to be built, you'd scarcely know it.

I explained to him my aborted meeting, our intentions of letting the inhabitants decide. He was amused:

— People like you, you buy two bottles from me just to ask if there's something interesting in the old village or the New City, and I say no, it's ghastly. But from now on I'll send them to you.

Two weeks later we held the first meeting in his kitchen: two young married couples, eventually interested, and for the rest, some inhabitants of the village itself.

The Meetings

Someone said: 'I'm going to talk to Gaby' (the mayor), and the second meeting took place in the town hall. We wished to meet the mayor without passing by the administration of the New City with whom he was in conflict: now he would no longer confuse us with it since we were 'from the village'. Then we spent a Sunday morning in the market of Cergy-Pontoise to explain to passers-by how we took account of and listened to their intentions. Little by little, some took what we said to others and our list of invitations grew.

Certainly the inhabitants' intentions, existing or future, were never surprising: they were even easy to guess. By contrast, the *gravity* of these intentions we couldn't guess at or even have had accepted by the authorities. These intentions concerned at first the tragic separation between the new installations and the ancient village, marked by the very sharp differences between the architecture, forms, tex-

tures, etc. and by a strongly resented lack of communication between the two zones, especially the car and pedestrian zones, and equally by a lack of physical contact. The general plan installed a green zone between the old and new parts, a zone resembling the *zones sanitaires*, the empty zones surrounding colonial towns. The plan of the new town, well done from many points of view, was fatally egocentric; it spontaneously placed its centre of interest in the middle of its new installation, and as for respecting the existing neighbourhood, it avoided it and threw the latter off balance (that is part of the definition of South African apartheid).

The mayor's office realised that for the first time it was listening to inhabitants of the old village and of the future one amicably discussing their future relationships and building them together. That was a change from the conflicts where the villagers had blocked the new administration office with their tractors.

What Did They Propose?

Three movements: first, the landscaping intentions for the village towards our terrain: colours, forms, roofing, alignments (not the 'New City' Style). It was the assembled villagers who spoke to the eventual inhabitants.

Following this, the 'real inhabitants' closed themselves up, at first in their kitchen, then their living room, bedroom, finally on paper. It wasn't until after organising their interior that they

'looked out of their windows' and made the acquaintance of their neighbours. And then of their countryside, a third movement.

All this had been registered (for fear of our professional deafness), analysed and interpreted immediately by rough forms and general plans, then synthesised by our ethnological friend, Itu Gassel, who coordinated and appended it.

A rush of meetings (how to predict them?), distant expeditions (we didn't have the means to install an on-site agency). Following this, mobile models and overall plans.

Group Work on the Overall Plan: Procedure

1 Our proposition after what we had already heard of the inhabitants' suggestions, implantation left to chance, in order to encourage the inhabitants to adapt their own preferences.

2 In order to provoke debates, sudden well-ordered opposition.

3 'And if one made a little place with a bakery higher up, to tie in with the future neighbourhood.' And some streets and pedestrian paths. Differentiating the isolated and the group. Not the collective. Routes towards neighbours: they had been received by the mayor's office and had visited a few nearby existing detached houses.

4 Some private parcels, well cloistered: 'we're not Swedes'. Then the public place rather lower, towards the village: there already was one further up, this would tie in with the village.

One evening one of the inhabitants asked very officially: 'when are you going to proceed with the distribution of lots?' Answer: 'it is you who decide; install yourselves, then'. And each dashed towards the overall plan to mark his name on the coveted lot, like gold prospectors. Astonishing: there was no conflict, each one had chosen a different lot and then teased his neighbour for having chosen less well. One, at lot A7, placed himself in the middle of principal traffic (one had to detour around his parcel), another at the entrance of a cul-de-sac, two others twice removed behind those who bordered the street (they were two architectural couples who wanted to see without being seen, one found out later), a few above, a few below, a few on the edges, in the middle, etc. One had to turn all the parcels upside down in order to rearrange them.

Instinctive Urbanism

When people enter a room as a group, they situate themselves through rapport with others of a similar character near the exit, along the walls, near the window, towards the centre, turning their back towards others, in the corners, and even at the very back in order to see without being seen . . . It is this instinctive manner of situating oneself that creates the form of the group in its space, it is this which has created villages, important cities and ancient towns. From a fabricated urbanism, this no longer seems thinkable: we rediscovered it by chance, letting things happen, because it isn't contrived or provoked.

The definitive plan, other spaces formed themselves, the lots were turned over a little once more. Families installed themselves, the neighbourhood traded, designing or choosing

7-10 Site plans of

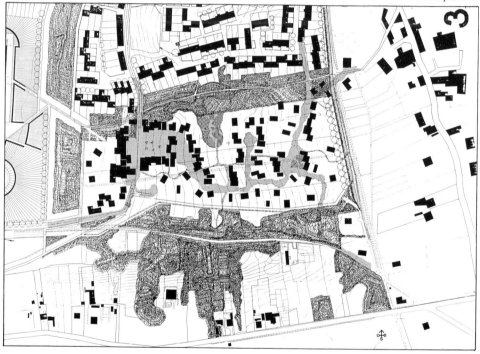

their models. Mister A7 definitely planted himself and consolidated all the smaller parcels of land step by step. And while no one had a desire any more to modify the overall plan, it became definitive even if all the details hadn't been resolved. The perimeter of the first phase had simply included the territory reserved for the 43 houses without the workings of logic.

What had we heard, interpreted and proposed? A greatly detailed configuration with streets, pathways, of squares and cul-de-sacs producing a strong differentiation of contexts, densities, neighbourhoods, types and volumes of lodgings (led by the typologies of the families, their ages and diverse occupations, even if the range wasn't very wide . . .).

Traffic Routes

The road system was no longer a ribbon but a space between houses or closures, a covering that engulfed the sidewalks in the same sheathing, without borders. The heavy route was marked out by paving stones placed in plots, their contour varying and responding to diverse situations and landscaping and, moreover, at a regularised distance from the axis. Traffic no longer impinged, pedestrians felt at ease. Landscaping amplified this.

During the course of the meetings, it was an inhabitant who proposed a connection with the autoroute below, on the network of our neighbours: we proposed it to the New City which then adopted it. A network of more closely

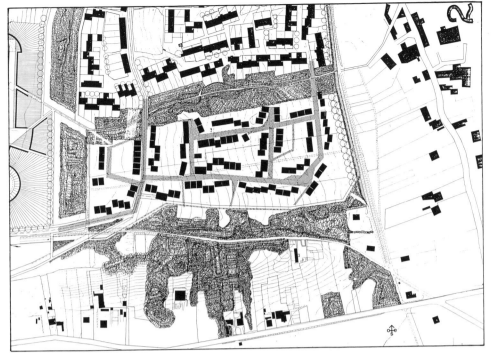

initial design proposals.

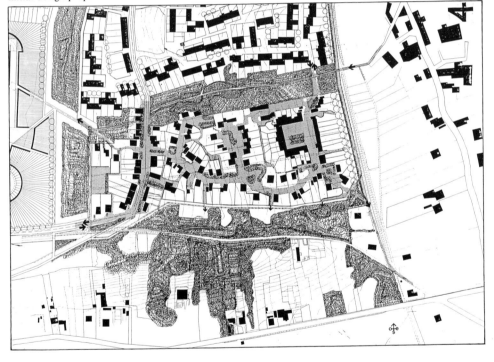

sense, the juxtapositions, the inequalities, finally all that which forms an urban texture, the absence of which attains only the level of a boarding school model or that of embellished barracks.

For lack of place, all our meetings were collective: at the beginning some were discreetly set aside for interviews with others. Then the participants got to know each other better, helped one another and created a collective dimension.

Seated with us in a café after one of the meetings, Mr C got up, excusing himself: 'look, there's Mr L passing by, I'll go say hello. He's my future neighbour.' That seemed normal, commonplace. Mr L worked in a nursery; if he saw any sick plants in public spaces, he would replace them as soon as possible.

Ecological Intentions
Some architectural students were sometimes invited, throwing into the discussion such themes as ecology, solar heating, of possible cooperatives, in general well received but thought too expensive. Apart from small vegetable gardens (but the terrain was rather scanty), we had above all proposed a general overgrowth of all possible plants, large and small trees, trailing plants for hard surfaces, on the hedges, etc. Apart from the regulation trees, we submitted to the inhabitants varying species, but their botanical knowledge was insufficient to raise a real discussion.

The gardens enterprise deceived us a bit, and we planted exotic species, now no longer sold. When we asked one of the inhabitants to replace them with familiar local species, he proposed to keep them: 'they're in Martinique, we'll call that country . . .'

The Stream
The water from the roofs was drained into a sort of stream/ditch, rather a string of small dams, slightly waterproofed, which could shelter more aquatic plants than elsewhere. At the bottom of the stream, it was too full towards the sewer. Some were enthusiastic, some feared that people would throw dirty papers into it. They were slightly mollified to recall that at least they would have the power to bank up the stream and to replace it with a pipe, since they formed a cooperative and managed their public spaces.

They had to rescue the authorisation for it from the city, then that was suddenly ineffectual: the water detoured by construction was not directed towards the stream. It is now a little vague terrain, incomprehensible.

A few amiable critics said about the organisers: 'this isn't self-management. And anyway, self-management isn't possible. Good. Because I've tried self-management in youth movements, university groups, my own students . . . I no longer have the energy to form new friendships with neighbours and to find myself alone again with all the responsibilities, no.' 'Besides,' added another, 'self-management that must respect all the laws and habits vigorously, that won't stand up. You see, I'm not even finishing the construction myself: someone will leave me out, some impediment will arrange that, etc . . .'

A very calm man, Mr A7, of Italian origin, came with his plan, very precise. He had chosen for himself the terrain in the centre, placing a

woven pedestrian routes was drawn up and incorporated in the plans. It was the inhabitants of the first phase who had protected the ensemble of three phases in general lines, then their lots in greater detail.

How did we find ourselves? Before tracing anything, wondering why that must be right (or even drawn . . .) or repeated? What was a rule, a mistake? One illusion to get rid of: this participation was not *laissez-faire* no matter what, no matter how. But before deciding or roughly imposing the organic solution, there was some difference (in our situation it wouldn't produce itself spontaneously any more). Following this, to propose a form that was both fertile and compatible: that was already architecture. It would

welcome the diversity of cultural images, by continuity, by contrast, occasionally by conflict but without annihilation. A compatible society. The artifice of property developers was insupportable, even a finishing that was well-composed or disguised under the cheap finery of classicism. The anti-establishmentarians of yesterday are the powers of tomorrow and are preparing themselves to be as annoying. It is no longer possible to model oneself on either commercial models or the heroic gestures of theoreticians. It does seem to us, however, legitimate to conserve through the maladroit reactions of groups the contradictions, the hesitations, the misfirings, the multiplications, the superimpositions, the piracies, the atavisms, the non-

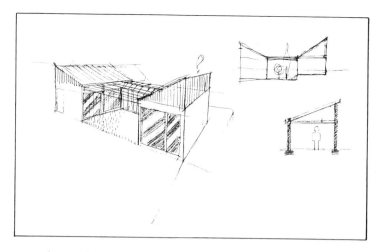
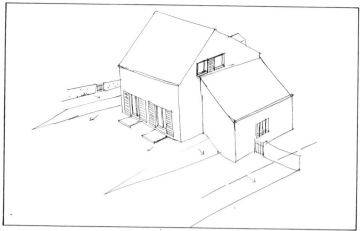

square house with a hipped roof, well isolated on its parcel, on it, 'inviolable'. 'That will be good, with a projecting cornice all around.' The facade faced fully south onto the street, not one window, only an entry door opened with a beaded curtain for flies as in Italy. Fundamentally, the colour traversed the house and gave over to the three metres of the garden (and not an Italianate landscape . . .). The rooms connected one to another (the model from his childhood). Hours of patient explanation with him, and as soon as one changed a few centimetres of his plan, he rectified it and took up again with an explanation: nothing remained but to amplify its character: we proposed to him a glass shelter over the entry door: 'Okay, with a lamp underneath . . .', and designs for panels on the front door: 'that will be prettier.' The garage door was on axis: with a majestic double staircase. The lavatory was ventilated by a window toward the bath. He verified it, it was good. Long isolated in the group, he only spoke to us. But when his plan was completley designed and evaluated, he looked around him from his central house and established relations: he proposed that his brother, an entrepreneur in Rome, come with a truck full of flagstone paving for his neighbours . . . Then some business disorder, suddenly he

could no longer finance his A7 lot but reserved another one facing the first to keep the view. Then he gave it up completely . . . sad.

A woman showed us a property magazine. 'That,' she said, showing a narrow and pretentious L-shaped villa, a dining room far from the kitchen, skylights, etc . . . Then on another page, the floor of another house. That would coincide. We worked with her to collate one with the other and to adapt it to the terrain. We manoeuvred it a little so that she would understand the rapport with her neighbours and surroundings. There remain an arched entry and a skylight.

Another couple wanted to live by day on the first floor and sleep on the ground floor. The husband, moreover, was impassioned with the idea of decorating the facade with rose sandstone. We were sure of a contagion toward the neighbours. Perhaps we should have been able to work the exterior plastering with the workers, the inhabitants, the children, to give more poetic importance to the entry doors and to certain windows by playing with the thicknesses of paint coats, the edgings, the stoneware recesses, etc. It didn't succeed; too much, too costly.

On-Site Employment
Certain purchasers wanted to practise their

employment on their lots: an industrial designer, a painter, an architect. At once the presence of local professionals broke the monotonous homogeneity of the residents and added to it a richness of different proportions. How to provoke it from the beginning? It was suggested to invite a doctor, a nurse, but how to lure them? Equally, where was the boutique seller who would sell everything, or a few older couples who would play the role of fond grandparents?

The Developer
It was only after we had led the first meetings ourselves and proposed the first general plans that a developer – whose role had been to start up, organise and manage cooperatives until the end of construction – became interested in the operation. A little official self-management. But we often went to the construction sites, because although the developer knew about cooperatives, he had forgotten cooperation. For reasons of his own ease or from fear of the co-operators, he remained as distant as possible and saw them only as ordinary buyers of a commercial product. The obligatorily opened books were clearly too complicated and so were closed. The developer nearly always responded to a question but at great length, and he took offence when

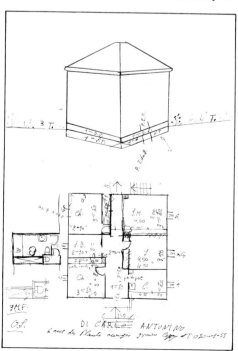
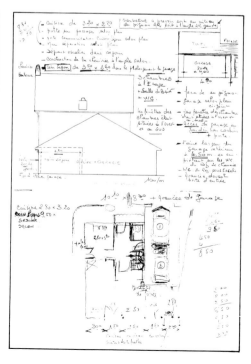

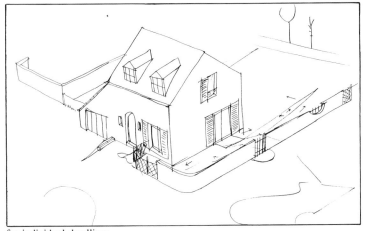

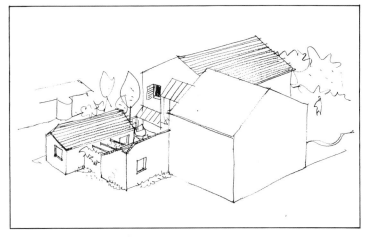

for individual dwellings.

someone got angry at a meeting. One day we asked him to distribute someone's address to everyone: 'you're crazy,' he said, 'they'll meet him.' Used to mechanical operations, some of the inhabitants' awkwardness provoked such a retort that altercations began. In effect, one knew that during the six months between the first really significant meetings and the decisions about the beginning of construction, the people would become discouraged, the group would break up and it would be very difficult to complete it. That, unhappily, happened to us: the developer didn't really believe in this manner of doing things and wanted only to fall back on his bad habits.

We had always refused to change the houses designed or modified by inhabitants, even those who left; they had to be sold such as they were to new inhabitants. It was never necessary to erase the traces of the former inhabitants but rather add new intentions to them. In this way, certain houses were redesigned by three or four successive families and they conserved all these sedimentary beds of intentions. One obstinate misunderstanding: we were neither sociologists nor nurses. So much the better if families or individuals bloomed on these occasions but that wasn't our purpose. We tried simply to lead

them towards an architecture which wouldn't prevent their way of life, which came into being by following their initiatives and which produced an image of realised pluralist responsibilities. We were not charged with the constitution and the health of the group of inhabitants (even if we were sensitive to it) but with creating with them and with craftsmen an architecture visibly more cooperative than usual. We had to repeat this every time other cooperators attached themselves to us.

No longer did we have to impose 'architectural care' on frustrated people. So much better, too, if they restructured a family pattern or even an active political implication, but that wasn't our goal. Neither was an amateurish put-up job and its ill-formed folklore.

Evolution

At Vignes Blanches, the inhabitants had the right to add annexes of up to fifty per cent of their initial surface (in all other operations the fixity of the architecture forbade it). And if too little time hastened the course of construction, the inhabitants themselves could add the shutters they weren't able to pay for at the start, and in several more diverse ways than what we would have been able to do. The fencing and plantings

were not achieved: the inhabitants began it afterwards and helped one another in the interior of their district. One kind of architectural aid would be to get the most important tasks into working order.

Commercial Arguments

Our developer-foreman of the cooperative at first very feebly interested himself in our approach, his feelings ranging from mistrust to effrontery; our approach seemed only exotic to him, a financial and commercial difficulty. He hung onto his habits: heavily analysing a market, badly guessing the demand, blindly translating it into a few idiotic models that tried to be 'alluring', then developing a gross commercial effect in order to get rid of the 'product' and risk having to finance it for a few months or years . . . And without costly trademarks or sale offices, with only two or three discreet announcements, almost all 43 houses were already inhabited on paper before construction. Everything sold better than usual.

We aimed at serial construction, not made to measure (even if . . .), within the limits of actual procedures and in order to show that all the operations could be diversified in a banal fashion, repeated. (But it still wasn't proved . . .)

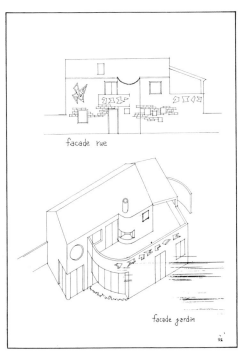

facade rue

facade jardin

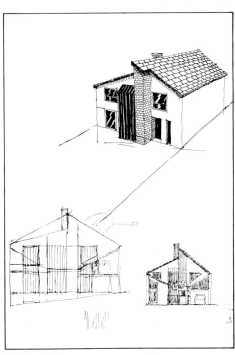

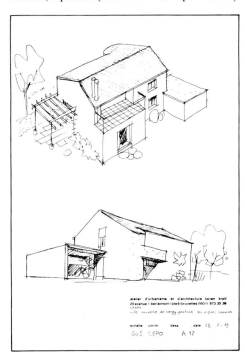

21,22 Aerial perspective and site plan of final design.

Better to single out mental laziness before complexities, the real costs. For example, a very disordered planting struck fear at first sight but in any case no more could be spent on it.

In some rather calculated prices, the least cost factor was strongly marked: houses (smaller than others), use of materials, dislocated volumes, difficulties of construction or site, and understandably, better-chosen materials. One must confess that in order to respect budgets, we had at our disposal a slightly compromised construction which consisted of badly stacking breeze blocks, coating them, isolating them, putting them on a thin concrete flooring, a very tight framework in the trusses, ordinary rooftiles and standardised windows... The least divergence was costly – but was it perhaps this that created the materials and traditional popular arts of former times?

We were able to negotiate the market with a small business group and to calmly discuss its prices over several months. Other larger groups had asked us: 'how many different models of the 43 buildings?' We answered: 'Forty-three.' They replied: 'No.'

Significance

We lost that slightly colonial certainty of controlling the whole creation of the built object, of controlling the total design in the manner of preceding generations of architects and planners. By contrast, we often had the occasionally annoying feeling of following a process that we didn't know well, the pictures of which only became apparent after the fact (like heaps of ruins where the logic of the plan is revealed only at a distance). Each time we passed near an ordinary building plot, we asked ourselves the same question: 'what difference has come out of our participation in Vignes Blanches? Perhaps the form produced by this sort of urban script, automatic and collective, that we raised, perceived and manoeuvred? Wouldn't it be better to be ignorant about how the action may end than to construct a too well known object, limited to itself?

23-26 Detail elevations and plans of final design.

Always two tracks. On the one hand, the troop and rank, the sublime, the complacent and no longer rational leaders, driving back, even retrogressing, glacial. On the other hand (and it really is the other hand), the unknown of personal and group initiatives (and that risks being ugly!), the diversity which alone can allow popular instincts to peacefully develop today, the certainty that the organic is more fertile than the calculated But inspiration is necessary: a generation of know-it-alls has frozen inhabitants.

To order is a military act: to motivate is to be responsive and responsible. And then, friendly relations. 'They' know nothing. Models all done! Disorder. And the architectural act? And corporatism? Populism, kitsch, and not the responsibility of the architect?

What can one gain as an architect? Adherence to a more palpable reality, saying nothing about our desires to determine everything alone. Co-production of an image of a more lively network, escaping to a type of machinist architecture without resorting to the travesties of the eighteenth century or to annoyingly narcissistic or Mussolini-style engineers. In this sense, while a plastic dwarf or a flat tyre may appear, it's a sign of better health than the emptiness of great inert schemes . . .

All or Nothing?

We were reproached about this by purists who demanded (from other people, because they themselves would attempt no participation) if the participants at the beginning would be the same ones at the end of the operation: we would have thought so. But while the more personalised houses were sold first (the 'rogues', said the developer, who demanded that we replace them by 'models'), we saw that the city was already transformed by successive inhabitants, often even before being built, and that this dimension made a more collectivist texture than a collage of personal preferences.

And from a few other purists, the inverse reproach was simultaneously directed at us: the inhabitants had been manipulated by the

architects. They were evidently right, but forgot that in exchange the inhabitants manipulated us also. They were certainly wrong to imagine that if we had been mute photocopiers the inhabitants would have designed houses in the shape of Mickey Mouse or boots. Not there. They projected their own myths: the real inhabitants showed themselves more responsible and more careful (we often regretted it . . .). We often received angry letters with a list recommending urgent modifications: for the most part, 10 cm here, moving back the furniture there, don't budge the radiator, nothing spectacular. Once that was corrected, they really felt at home. And then, without vigorous architects they would have simply repeated the immediate models and the bleak alignments of lots which one believes inevitable, so much so that one excavates only in the shameful motifs of engineers and geometricians . . .

Alas, if one can ardently hope for inhabitants, if we finally leave them to organise themselves, they could continue to realise their initiatives . . . But by a curious misunderstanding, it isn't the inhabitants one listens to but those who make a profession of knowing better than they do.

Entropy

The vague participation which had overtaken the New City finally produced only a few things. Since 1976, several operations were debated in Cergy before getting bogged down. The first, vigorously led by a solid developer, didn't want to plunge into the experience without preparation and constructed about a dozen models which the future inhabitants could choose and modify as they pleased. But in the face of the reticence and slowness of possible buyers, the developer decided to multiply these 12 models without anything more and to sell them like cattle trucks . . .

Another experience, this one very successfully passing its first phase, was that of the *Ateliers Communautaires* (Community Workshops); they put several years into dispensing

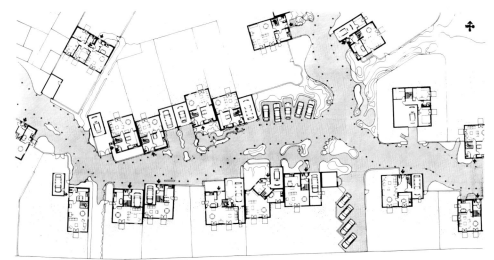

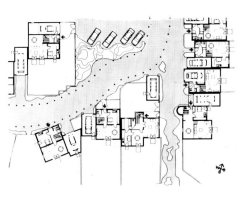

with developers, into researching their own purchasers, into redrawing their statutes, into working directly with them and changing contracts with businesses forming a cooperative founded for this reason. They actually struggled, eight years later, in the second phase of the operation, for which it seemed that there weren't enough buyers or somehow they weren't 'caught' or somehow the economic circumstances weren't favourable enough.

We were the third operation, chronologically, perhaps it was because of the dislocation and disorder of our first developer that we succeeded in obtaining a rather strong participation but with very long delays and a great waste of meetings.

And then, element by element, the intentions of the inhabitants were suppressed by the developer. At first the bakery (it isn't our role), then the community hall (it makes noise) and the work places, then certain varieties of materials and colours (costing more), finally a few of the older couples, and finally no more participation, not even the arrangement of the third phase of 'operation Vignes Blanches'. If it had been well led by a competent developer it wouldn't have cost any more time or money. But entropy . . .

Commonplace Community

This operation at Vignes Blanches had a remarkable characteristic: it wasn't a group made up of inhabitants who sought a communal habitation in order to shut themselves up in it, it was an open operation no matter what, where no one

was chosen or refused, where no privilege was necessary to belong. Our inhabitants came from it didn't matter where, they simply wanted to live there without any other care except a very light communal one, to build good neighbourly relations: without obligation, without constraint, without rights over others heavier than those which were like any other urban district. Truly anyone could be integrated into this district provided that material conditions were satisfied.

These characteristics seemed essential to us because they distinguished us from other communitarian ventures, religious, political, intellectual, etc, which had been made to deviate from this notion of participating in the architecture of one's habitat, deviating from an indispensible banality, towards a mystique of communal obligation more or less manipulated or organised by 'charitable' specialists. Banality protected us from these suffocations, from these nostalgias for ancient forms of society and at the same time from that kind of architecture which produces authoritarian relations between the group and the people; banality protected us from the complicity of architecture with communal homogeneity: that is the difference between a boy scout troop and the bustling crowd of the market place . . .

This is not a criticism of communal or homogeneous architecture but simply a research with another object. This is a normal repeatable process, in no matter what contemporary circumstance, that by itself helps the urban tissue

to grow and only avoids those 'building mercenaries' who immediately transform architecture into their technical or cultural image.

Success?

Despite conflicts, we were lucky to have a maladroit developer, sometimes well motivated, sometimes not; his lack of experience in participation (despite his role as organiser of cooperatives) simply left us alone: we were able to mollify him just enough in order to start the operation: he could no longer stop it. We see now that with a better organised and more solid developer, these attitudes probably would have been impossible. Or indeed, maybe it takes an innocent organiser, competent and angelic, but does one exist?

Despite the delays and dislocations, we feel that this operation had a certain commercial success: everything was sold and even faster than usual. We have to keep telling ourselves that an operation where open participation completely miscarried is still only one ordinary operation . . .

The little group of 43 families now live their lives. We returned there for the pleasure of it, even if there were many problems and minor faults badly resolved. We were on the watch for all personal developments and fixtures: there were several all around. Gardens had been organised, we found tomato plants in the ambiguous public gardens. Fencing grew everywhere, copying our forms (or even better, they tried to rectify them), people came, improving

the built reality.

the public spaces, sometimes privatising them, enlivening them, adding a few open sheds, a few awnings, a few annexes towards the gardens. They were often in each others' gardens, without avoiding neighbourly disputes. One of them worked in the business of concrete casting and showed me a model in classic form of a balcony railing that he had made for his terrace. I said, 'It's very good.' He proposed them to his neighbours: contagion. The house designed to the millimetre by the artisan of Italian origin who wasn't able to follow through had been repurchased by a Swiss couple, then by another couple. It changes every week.

One will have to return in twenty-five years.

Conclusions

This operation had been a difficult wager towards an ethnology. We decided at first to put aside our personal style, and to adopt, not blindly but in friendship, the local banal style and the 'bad taste' of popular actors. Certainly we had our personal limits but they were enlarged by the wager: certain propositions we didn't support, others we didn't perceive (our selective deafness . . .).

In all ways, from the beginning we projected a personal model but one which was undefined, more like an attitude; the model was then built progressively from discussions, was nourished by arguments and culminated in an organic form. This model was made from complexities, from non-repetitions and from a refusal to let a

hard form dominate the landscape. It was inscribed by the inhabitants, it became their material and finally their architecture. It wasn't *laissez-faire* no matter who or what or how but it was closer to the democracy that respects everyone (and throughout centuries, villages were admirably formed in this fashion). It was no longer a matter of designing one sole project, then manipulating the inhabitants so that they accept it. It was surely the two motifs, simultaneously. In this way one understands that with fewer inhabitants, one may have decided everything, and then all the projects would have resembled each other!

Equally one understands that the architecture of the first phase wasn't really different from that of the second or third, the detail of which was made without a single inhabitant. And that here, imitation was finally closer to the model and that attitude was more sincere than action. It is very difficult to do the decorative artifice since we wanted neither an angelic spontaneity nor a foreign object. We forced artifice to be a tool: we ourselves were artifice . . .

Our approach was above all that of the landscapist, therefore overall, relational, and of long duration. We say 'landscape' in the sense of a complex milieu constructed by decisions that intersect, are multiple and woven, never by rules that are rigid, 'right', or simplistic. Our approach was of long duration since we considered the past, the existing, the unsaid, like a texture upon which one sets a new project which is only one moment in history and which will continue to

evolve without us. Certainly this distanced us as much from other fabricators of artificial objects (High Tech or Walt Disney) as from equally artificial 'Roman' travesties (even if occasionally we had unconfessed sympathies with one or the other, if they were well done . . .).

This explains why we immediately turned the road systems upside down, the drainage system, the public spaces and their cunning authority over the landscape. Happily, here, we had an excellent and competent design team (and we often argued . . .). A dislocated road system permitted other spatial arrangements, other landscapes.

The form of Vignes Blanches is slightly 'animal', 'instinctive', with the necessary crudeness. The houses possess a necessary banality and the games of chance of volumes involuntarily meeting (this upsetting was desired, not the detail of its effects). As soon as they entered their houses, the inhabitants began to improve them: it was well decided.

We rarely saw any other artificially organised place that developed with this natural quality. And I don't believe we'll find any other similar circumstances that would allow us to go as far with active inhabitants. Here we already needed the friendly protection of the New City and the mayor of Jouy, and the ministerial subsidies to get there, because it's sometimes exhausting to persuade interventionists to act naturally . . .

Translated by Christine Murdock

SITE

THE FRANKFURT MUSEUM OF MODERN ART

Programme Requirements

Note: This project was developed as a competition entry by SITE, sponsored by the Municipal Government of Frankfurt for a new Museum of Modern Art. The specifications were as follows:

1 The designated site is a triangular intersection flanked by three major streets, presently occupied by a municipal parking lot. The museum itself is part of a new cultural development programme in Frankfurt which will include a series of large exhibition facilities over the next few years.

2 As background information it is important to remember that Frankfurt was 90% destroyed by bombing raids during the Second World War and, with the exception of the cathedral and some of the buildings on Braubachstrasse, virtually the entire city has been rebuilt. There is a central commercial area of high-rise offices and the rest is mostly 18 metres high domestic architecture from the 1950s in stucco or masonry.

3 The museum itself must conform to the site, not exceed 18 metres in height, and include a 60° setback after 18 metres.

4 The new museum structure must respect the character of the neighbourhood – especially the domestic architecture of Braubachstrasse – but it should also be a dramatic focal point in the neighbourhood and a 'gateway' project to the city as a whole.

5 The Director of the new Museum of Modern Art has defined his objectives as establishing a building which is dramatic and expressive on the exterior and extremely simple and flexible on the interior. He has further described the structure as an industrial warehouse for the storage and exhibition of art, but also a place for such expanded art forms as video and performance. The ambience of the museum should be a showcase to both exhibit and encourage experimentation in the visual arts.

6 The foundation of the museum's permanent collection is American art of the 1960s and 1970s (with an emphasis on Pop Art).

7 Natural light is important, but energy efficiency must be respected.

8 Interior circulation must function as a cohesive and flexible programme and the general ambience should suggest a museum that is democratic and community-oriented.

9 Since the site area is wanting in vegetation, it has been deemed desirable but not mandatory to include a garden space.

Concept Description

For practical and philosophical reasons, SITE decided to place a rectangular building on a triangular site. From a functional standpoint, this concept avoids the problem of creating awkward interior spaces typical of triangular

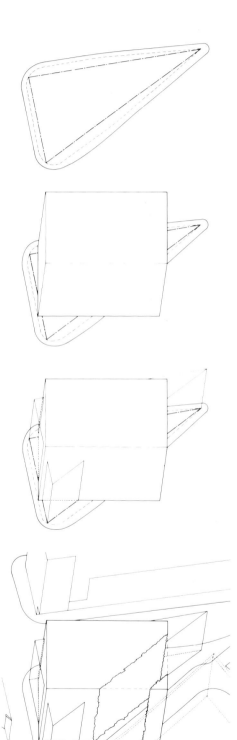

1 Concept drawings.

structures. From an aesthetic perspective, this denial of the site is a rejection of the standard celebration of the triangle which would have been a more conventional tactic.

The concept evolved in the following four stages:

The first stage is the graphic definition of the site area.

The second procedure is to insert a rectangular building (or, the actual museum enclosure), with a north/south/east/west orientation consistent with the other major public buildings in Frankfurt.

Since it is necessary for the spectator to be aware of the triangular site configuration in order to understand the invasion of the rectangle, the site area is defined by an abstraction of it in glass (18 metres high, supported by a space frame) which penetrates the masonry structure of the museum. This enclosure also functions as a café and sculpture garden.

When this ensemble of interpenetrating structures is placed on the actual site, it becomes necessary to sever one corner of the rectangular museum facing Braubachstrasse in order to allow the street to pass freely. Rather than design this incision in a geometric and formalistic way, the convention of the rough architectural cutaway is used to create a more intense dialogue between exterior and interior.

Philosophical Notes

The SITE concept for the Museum of Modern Art in Frankfurt is a visual dialogue about positive and negative, inside and outside as fundamental architectural issues. It is also an inversion of the traditional notions of 'site definition', since the idea essentially denies the triangular configuration; but then resurrects it as a vertical memory or abstraction of the site. By violating the site, it is redefined as a new site.

The project is a dialogue between disparate and conflicting elements, between two buildings – one a functional structure for occupancy and the other an ephemeral enclosure without practical intentions.

The mass of the masonry building establishes a dialogue between German and American culture, since the museum houses what is essentially an American art collection. It is the prototypical Germanic factory style that invaded the United States in the nineteenth century and still dominates certain regional industry to this day. It also, as a building type, recalls the fact that virtually all American art of the past twenty years was produced in similar structures in the Soho section of New York City.

2 Perspective.

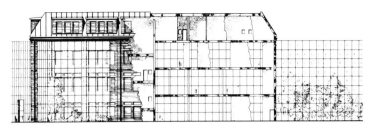

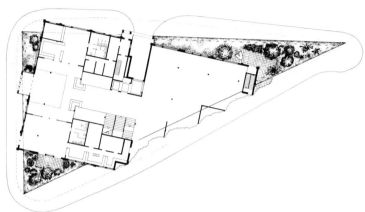

3, 4 Section and plan

At the same time, the interpenetrating glass enclosure can be read as a tribute to the work of Mies van der Rohe and the Bauhaus – and, again, the international influence of German architecture.

As in all of SITE's work, architecture becomes the 'subject matter' of an art-making process. In this case, the familiar typologies of industrial masonry building, mansard roof, and large dormers are retained as the essential conventions to be recycled as the raw material for a series of layered transformations. This conceptual layering of ideas *about* architecture (as opposed to 'designing' architecture), becomes the entire source of the museum's meaning and its integration with the surrounding community. Whereas, for example, Post-Modernism has used historically referenced decorative devices to increase communication and add richness of surface to buildings, the surface complexities of SITE's Frankfurt Museum derive from these stratified ideas, rather than from applied decoration.

By not conforming to the triangular site, the masonry building is arbitrarily severed on the south side to accommodate Braubachstrasse. In this sense, the Braubachstrasse elevation serves as a metaphor for the Second World War bombing of the city, as an architectural cutaway convention made into a physical reality, and as a dialogue between exterior and interior.

The glass enclosure serves as both a physical and graphic representation of the site. In some cases – for example, the major stair landings – the space frame support penetrates the masonry from exterior to interior, with dramatically sculptural results. On the other hand, the more conceptual illustration of the triangular site is accomplished with a dotted line (to be either engraved in the flooring or woven into the carpet surfaces. This dotted line convention will always be used in the interiors to identify the existence of the triangle.

The SITE museum serves as an appropriate shelter for a permanent collection of revolutionary visual art by including many of the ideas and issues which inform these works – for example, inversion, irony, humour, social and environmental commentary, and the redefinition of art.

The project serves as both a monument and an anti-monument. Although the building does not address any particular social or ideological issue, it does offer a commentary on the nature of architecture and context, rhetoric and traditions, site planning, and the role of the museum in the community. In view of the fact that one of the basic requirements in the prospectus for the competition was a 'democratic museum', this anti-institutional character should help to make it more accessible to the community and international visitors to Frankfurt.

Since Frankfurt is identified in Europe as a leading international centre of commerce and liberal thought, this museum should serve the image well. Although designed to integrate with its context in terms of appropriate image and scale, the structure is not provincial in any sense of the word. Its universal conceptual premises make it an accurate reflection of the community.

Description of Interior Spaces and Services
The first floor exhibition space represents the essence of the concept of the museum as a community-oriented, democratic, evolutionary experience. It also demonstrates the virtues of placing a rectangular structure on a triangular site, since all of the enclosed services – bookstore, security zone, coatroom offices, cafe, elevators, etc – fit into accommodating right-angle spaces, while the triangle affects only the main open gallery area where it is least intrusive.

To increase the dialogue between exterior and interior and create a street-view 'memory' of the rectangular building, the paving of the ground floor gallery extends outside into Braubachstrasse as a definition of where the missing corner of the museum once stood. This 'invisible' or 'ghost' image of the building is an extension of glass wall-as-site abstraction established by the enveloping triangle.

The main entrance of the museum is created by extracting the brick doorway portal, setting it out in alignment with the edge of the property line, and leaving the negative cutout of its contour as the actual entrance to the main lobby. In summary, every device is used to make the museum interior a part of the community, but at the same time to treat the exhibition space as a cultural sanctuary, free of the distractions of the street.

Consistent with the 'art in process' theme of the museum, all gallery interiors are designed to reflect a factory-like atmosphere, a place where works of art can be both exhibited and manufactured. To increase the flexibility of the space, a number of the walls function as cabinets to contain temporary exhibition panels and most of the ceiling areas support mechanized horizontal panels which can be raised and lowered. As a result of these facilities, the exhibition spaces can be altered to any size, shape or height needed for art installations.

To heighten the drama of entry to the museum, there is a vertical atrium between the ground and first floors. This provides museum visitors with an overview of the lobby and the opportunity to observe both people in transit and the temporary exhibitions.

A monumental stairway links all floors and each landing provides ample exhibition space for the permanent collection and special small shows.

SITE
PAZ BUILDING, BROOKLYN

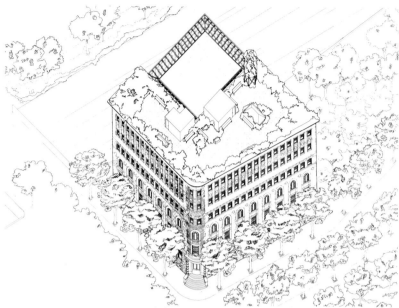

1 Aerial perspective.

Programme

The scope of the project includes the conversion of an existing 1904 YMCA building in Williamsburg to multi-use commercial space – including a restaurant, health facility, bank, and offices. Interior space will be expanded by the addition of a new 20,000 sq. ft. glass and steel enclosure on the east side, facing the Brooklyn/ Queens Expressway.

Concept Description

The SITE concept was developed in response to the client's desire to have this converted building stand as a gateway project, symbolising Williamsburg's dynamic state of renewal and its unique blend of cultures.

Although the structure is to be used for com-

mercial purposes, SITE felt that its imagery should reflect the general spirit of the community, with its conditions of contrast. For example, such themes as old/new, decay/rebirth, worldly/ religious, and closed/expansive seem to be more visually evident in Williamsburg than in any other New York area neighbourhood.

In order to both structurally and psychologically create an architectural presence for this duality, the new office building has been designed to emerge from the old YMCA centre as if by means of some miraculous resurrection. This will be accomplished by cutting away sections of the existing gymnasium wall on the east elevation facing the Brooklyn/Queens Expressway, leaving a raw-edged masonry profile. The addition of a glass and steel tower will rise out of

this fragmented contour, providing additional floorspace and a multi-level terrarium garden.

These re-birth and duality themes will be carried throughout the exterior, interior, adjacent gardens, and parking facilities. Interior decorative details remaining from the original YMCA design will be preserved and integrated.

The two major concrete portals located on the Marcy Avenue side of the old building will be re-cast into duplicates and inserted on the east elevation as a way of unifying historical references, alluding to the House of Abraham (with its four welcoming entrances), and establishing a symbolic point of entry to Williamsburg for the outside world.

2,3 Views of the existing YMCA Building west elevation and from the Brooklyn/Queens Expressway.

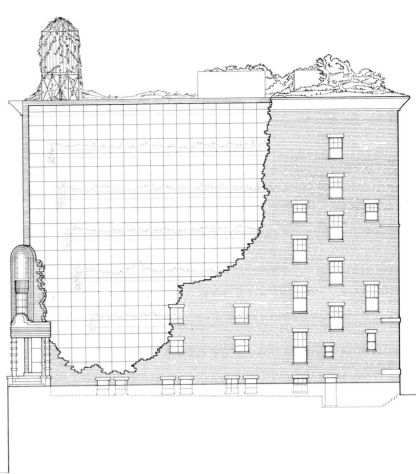

5,6 Side elevation and plan.

COMMERCIAL SPACE

LOBBY

KITCHEN

BANK

RESTAURANT

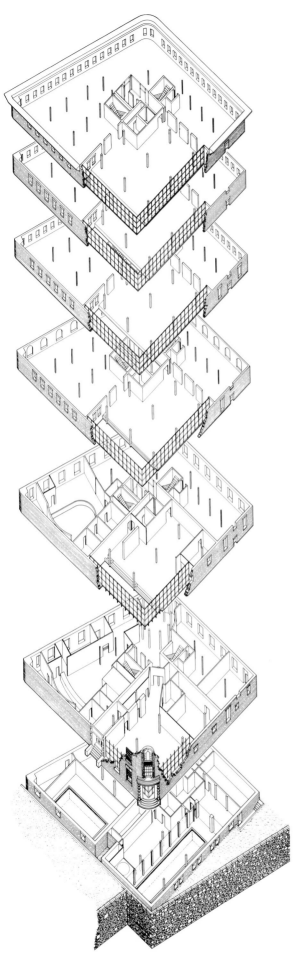

4 Exploded axonometric.

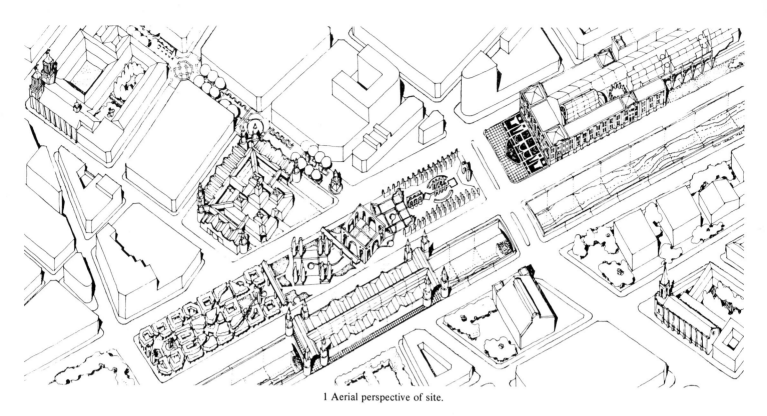

1 Aerial perspective of site.

2 Axonometric, plan and section of site.

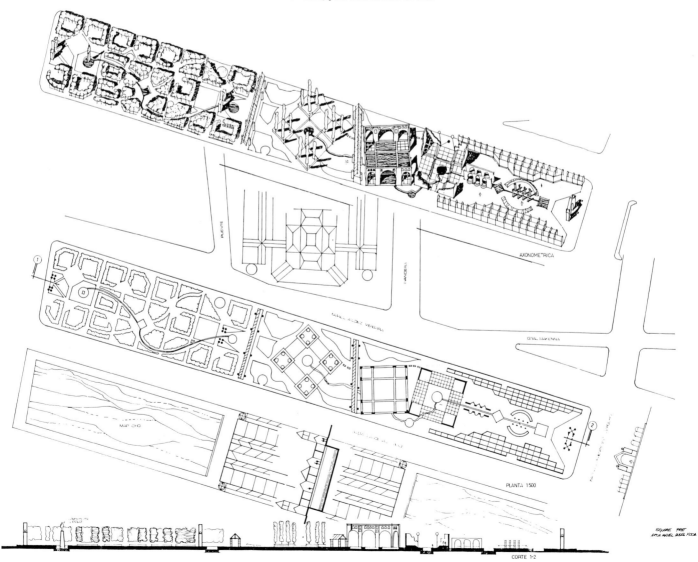

Miguel Angel Roca

CHILE MARKET–PRATT SQUARE–MAPOCHO STATION, SANTIAGO

Due to its privileged location, two blocks away from the Arms Square at the back of the Municipal Building and virtually on the same axis, the Santiago market, lying by the Mapocho, is the popular epicentre of the central area. Lying alongside the river, Mapocho Station together with the market defines an area of social, commercial, existential and even poetic richness and vitality.

Both are a northern gate of entry into the central area, an access from the north of the 'chimba' of the popular classes, with their vegetable markets, etc. The old, end-of-the-century market appears in its formidable cast-iron ornamented splendour, housing plain fish and handicraft stalls which have multiplied across thirty years, extending in a sort of crust five times their original capacity, distorting and oversaturating it until it is difficult to appreciate its value as an architectural heritage.

The strategy contemplates:
1 Maintaining the fish market activity by means of collective memory and the presence of the people in the central area;
2 Recovering the valuable structure and restoring it, emphasising it as a meeting centre, divesting it of the confusion of tiny stalls, exalting the periphery with gastronomic and handicraft stalls and the central area as a meeting square and covered communal centre.
3 Demolishing the accretions and rebuilding these in a light, unencumbered metallic structure in the shape of combs or packages of similar stalls internally connected by a glazed, U-shaped gallery embracing and exalting the old building, with a 6 metre continuous green

strip separating the old from the new to mark the difference and show at the same time its correlation.

The U-shaped perimeter building contains the monument and opens the complex towards the river, tensing it, together with the rest of the market area on the opposite bank. Special shop premises are lodged in six towers which, paraphrasing the San Francisco facade and the theme of the Chiloé churches, frame the corners like great doors in the complex. Out of the present 200 stalls 100 remain and the rest are rehoused in a bridge-like building with similar doors and structures, articulating both banks and defining the above-mentioned square opposite the market and the Mapocho station. Stressing the river axis as well as the building's integral wholeness is a central gallery space. Pratt Square becomes park-like, as if given the finishing touches of the one developing from the end of the nineteenth century as a forest park, with a present-day project of extending it as far as the north-south highway. This prolongation covering the present railway lines will include the building, following the example of the Palace of Fine Arts farther up the river.

This space, confronted with the urban protagonists of greater significance in the surroundings, takes its configuration laws from these. Facing the Market is a replica of it, reduced to the bare elements and component principles. A series of versions in greenery, in plaster, in water, commit and qualify the space towards the station. Pavilion-buildings with multiple metallic domes compose the trunks of those trees called creepers, describing an enclosure which

leads to the railway station.

A green chessboard garden miniaturises Santiago at the other end, appearing as a microcosm of the metropolis, as a synthesis of the natural border and the urban, physical phenomenon. This complex is proposed as rounding off the Ahumada pedestrians' mall and the bridge, another proposed design.

The railway station, a metallic structure with great lights of an unquestionable value, is completed with an entrance body in noble Renaissance style, and two lateral office bodies, at present abandoned. The project of removing the station (unified with the central one), is an imaginative challenge to generate an environment of equivalent symbolic value and a new oneiric quality; this time not the journey towards the immediate but a complicity with the remote: the plan is to house the famous FISA (International Santiago Fair) here. Part of the park is taken up by temporary pavilions and the central space with an amphitheatre for conventions and permanent exhibition salons, iconographically read as the 'last train', its carriages denoting a journey in constant arrival or departure.

The lateral ground floors house stores and cafés which multiply the uses and complement the activity of the fair. Corporation and professional offices are found in the upper storeys, where structures and facades are respected and restored, serviced by pairs of staircases characterised in their developments as virtually independent promenades which exalt and activate the facades of the inner premises, thus promoted to the level of covered plaza as an extension of the outer area.

3 Site plan of Santiago showing the strategy of intervention for the area.

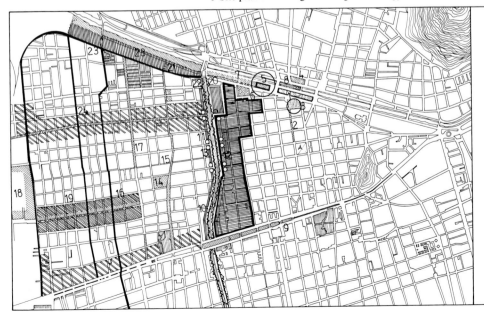

A MAIN SQUARE
1 Pratt Square
2 Calle Fuente pedestrian mall
3 Central market refunctionalisation
4 Vega central remodelling
5 Mapocho Station refunctionalisation
6 Prison refunctionalisation
7 Forest Square
8 Bridge Market
9 Avenue Alameda
10 Forest Avenue north/south
11 Parking
12 Commercial area
13 Commercial bridge
14 Brasil Square
15 Brasil Lane
16 Amplification of Avenue Portales
17 Cumming Lane
18 Quinta Normal Square
19 Intensification sector
20 Bus station
21 New Mapocho Station
22 Metro extension
23 Recreational square
24 North/south axis

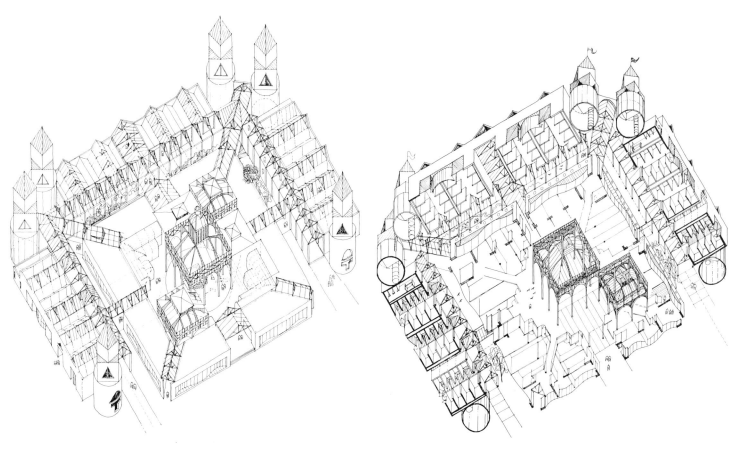

4-6 Bird's-eye and worm's-eye axonometrics, elevations and section of the Central Market.

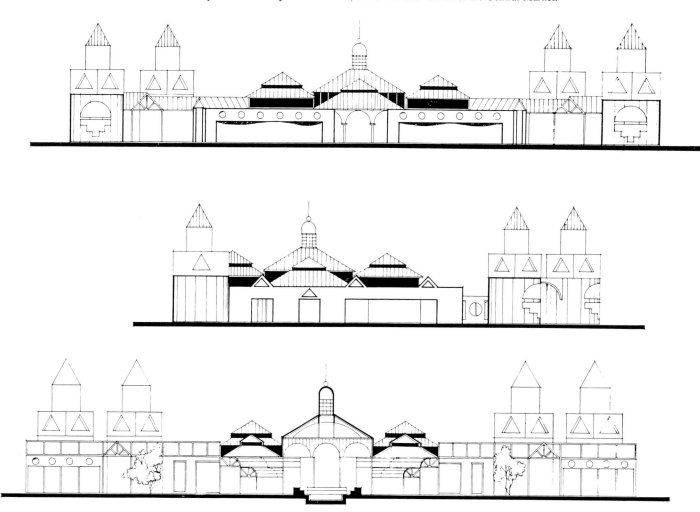

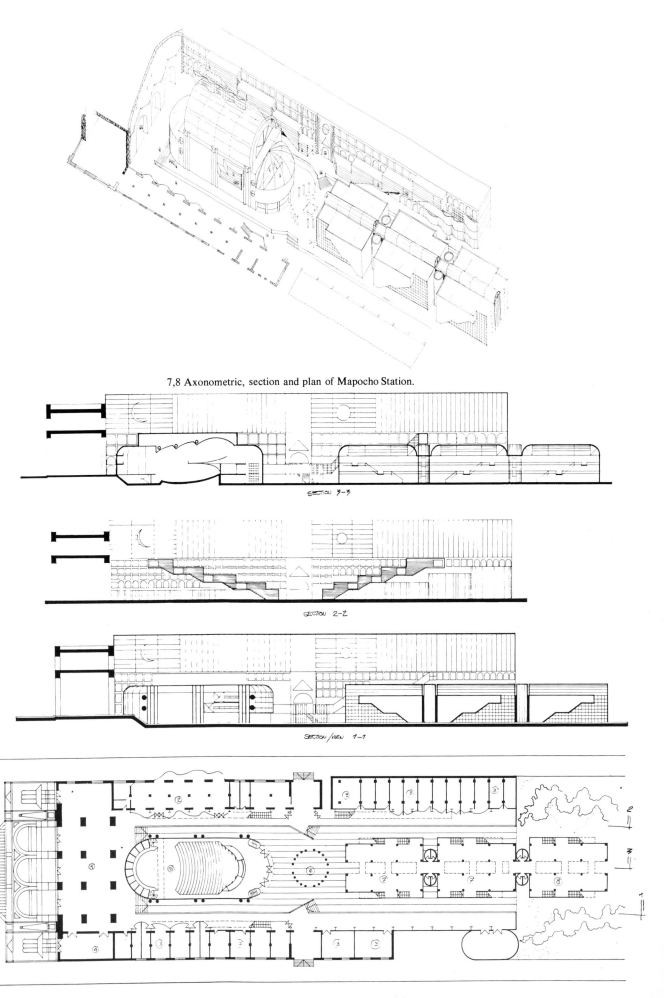

7,8 Axonometric, section and plan of Mapocho Station.

SECTION 3-3

SECTION 2-2

SECTION/VIEW 1-1

Emilio Ambasz
PLAZA MAYOR, SALAMANCA

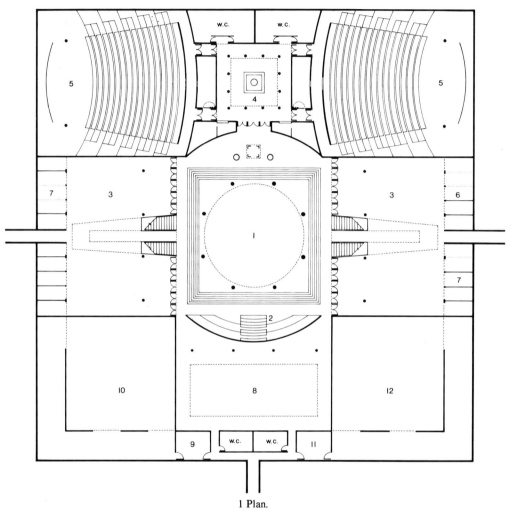

1 Plan.

A GARDEN IN THE CITY:
A CITY IN THE GARDEN

Salamanca:
Located in the middle of the Iberian peninsula, Salamanca is one of the oldest cities in Europe. Since 300 BC, Celts, Romans and Moors have conquered, destroyed and reconstructed the city. Boasting one of the oldest and most prestigious universities, Salamanca ranks with Bologna, Paris and London. The river Tormes supports a year-round green belt around Salamanca, making it an inviting bed for civilisation and distinguishing it from the frequently dry surroundings.

Plaza Mayor
In true Iberian fashion, the Plaza is the centre of Salamancan commercial and cultural activity as well as a place of repose: it is to the city what the city is to the surrounding province. Unobstructed, open and of square proportions, the Plaza stands

in contrast to the dense and irregular pattern of buildings and streets in the area. Facing directly over the plaza is a four-sided Baroque facade designed by Churriguera, which appears to be a continuous building due to the repetition of an equally spaced and detailed bay system. On the ground floor is an arcade, whose columns separate the various commercial and private interests from the open and public plaza.

The Project
The new city government wishes to improve this plaza. What is now a flat and barren plaza, unequipped for seating or gathering in very cold or warm weather, will become an inclusive space, shaded by trees. A series of concentric squares step down towards the centre, whose floor is a circular patterned metal grating lighting a dance hall directly below. The previous ground level of the plaza is maintained by the tops of the trees, creating a metaphorical ground cover of leafy clouds that float in the

middle of the plaza. As one descends into the plaza, the tree trunks begin to emerge from the pavement, increasing in height: columnar trunks and a green canopy overhead are reminders of the arcaded loggia seen beneath the surrounding buildings. Below the forested plaza are programmatic elements of a public nature: cinemas, theatres, gymnasiums, community offices, and in keeping with one of the traditional uses of the Plaza, the dance hall. The air pocket between the steps and these public functions acts as a plenum, using passive solar energy to cool the plaza in the summer when it is shaded, and to heat it in the winter when the leaves fall and it is exposed, allowing the sun to strike the stone steps.

Planted within Salamanca's walls and surrounded by her most civic architectural monument, the new Plaza Mayor grows physically as well as symbolically from the very stone of the city, offering a quiet and shaded retreat as well as a hub of public activity.

2,3 Perspectives of the plaza.

Emilio Ambasz
HOUSTON CENTER PLAZA

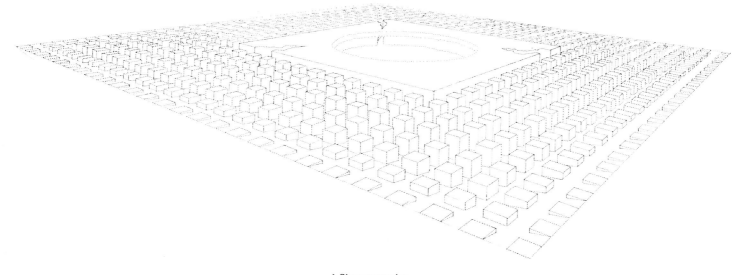

1 Site perspective.

The client requested a plaza which would provide an image for the city of Houston. The site is one of the square blocks typical of the overall grid organising the city. The block is to contain office buildings and a plaza with theatres, galleries and restaurants, connected to a convention centre on an adjoining block. The solution developed from a view of the plaza as a physical, a metaphorical, and a spiritual image of Houston.

The most outstanding feature of Houston is its square grid. It is a strength in that it permits endless expansion, but a weakness in that it does not allow for the definition of a well-defined centre. Yet it has potential since the purity of the grid may be used as a backdrop against which urban interventions may be read. Thus, the grid of the city was transformed into the grid of the plaza, with a rough edge on the outside representing the incomplete nature of the growing city, and the square pool in the centre representing the plaza in the city.

The plaza was also meant to represent various aspects of Houston on a metaphorical level. The culture of the city is represented by the theatres and the galleries; the commerce by the shops; the advanced technology by the laser exhibitions; the life and energy of the city by the life of the atrium which is at the heart of the shops and galleries.

Most important of all is the spiritual quality of the space. The outer part of the plaza consists of an array of trellises on a square grid covered by vines. The ground slopes down from the edge of the plaza to the large square pool in the centre with its circular opening above the atrium. The taller trellises toward the centre are like gazebos with portals and seating. All of the senses participate because of the colourful, fragrant flowers grown between the vines. Each enclosure has mist emanating from the top, thereby cooling the surroundings and producing a soothing hissing sound. The gazebos are places for relaxation from office work and from the heat of the city, places to talk to friends or places for quiet contemplation amid a green shade.

The sense of a cool retreat is reinforced by the water cascades around the square pool, the circular waterfall inside the pool, with its water continuing on as blades of water splashing in the atrium space. The entire effect is reminiscent of Islamic Moghul gardens: the play of the different sounds and textures of falling water, the lush vegetation, the colours, the fragrance, and the cool shade. This type of garden is appropriate for Houston because it was designed for a climate requiring the refreshment of water and shade, and also because it was designed as a contemplative, spiritual environment in keeping with a growing city.

This project excels as an urban scale solution which recognises its context on a local and a city level. The plaza provides a memorable and pleasant experience for the visitor, and it also provides a unified, complex image which richly represents the city of Houston on a physical, a metaphorical, and a spiritual level.

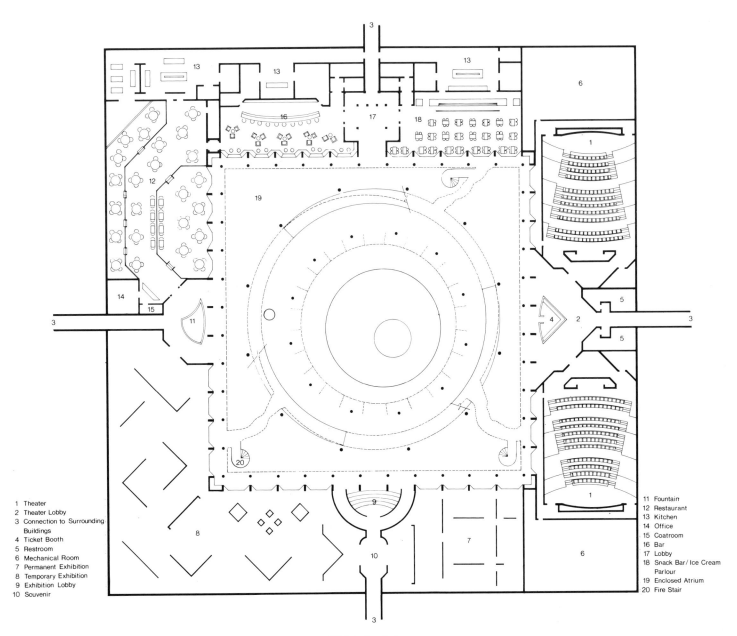

1 Theater
2 Theater Lobby
3 Connection to Surrounding
  Buildings
4 Ticket Booth
5 Restroom
6 Mechanical Room
7 Permanent Exhibition
8 Temporary Exhibition
9 Exhibition Lobby
10 Souvenir

11 Fountain
12 Restaurant
13 Kitchen
14 Office
15 Coatroom
16 Bar
17 Lobby
18 Snack Bar / Ice Cream
   Parlour
19 Enclosed Atrium
20 Fire Stair

2 Main level plan.

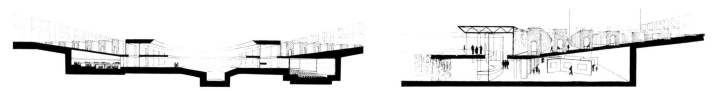

3-6 Site and exhibition area perspective sections.

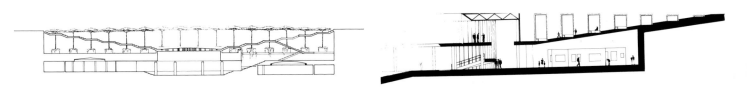

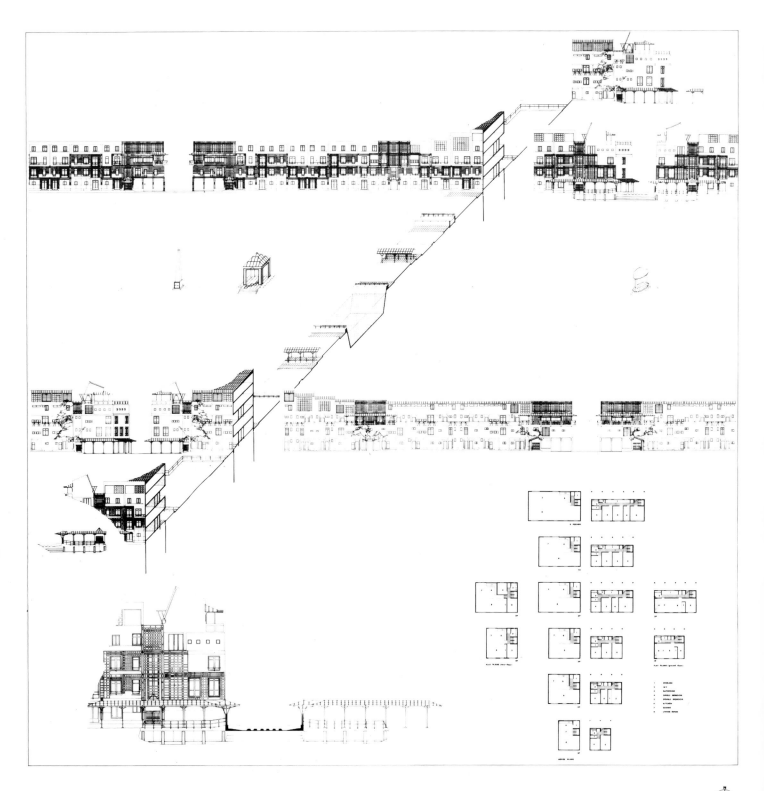

DWA 1982

1 Plans and elevations.

Derek Walker & Peter Barker
DOCKLANDS, ROTTERDAM

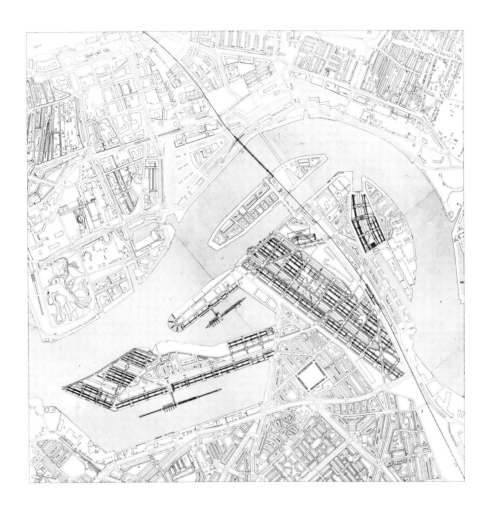

2 Site plan.

Derek Walker & Peter Barker
Assistants: Peter Salter, Bob Barnes

The invitation was to join in a limited competition to develop ideas for the reconstruction of a run-down docks area on the south-east edge of the commercial centre and river (the Nieuwe Maas) in Rotterdam. The area consisted to a large extent of derelict industry and semi-abandoned dock workings, but there remained in the area a significant number of those families, mainly of Dutch Indonesian and Afrikaner origin, which had provided the dock labour force before the relocation of the city's main commercial dock operations downstream to Europort.

The objective was the reassembly of a working community – industrial regeneration, new housing and commercial facilities and new schools. The brief called for around 9,000 new dwellings at an average household size of 2.5 persons and included a land allocation budget:

but the development brief and the area available for development were regarded as flexible.

The problem was to explore the structural characteristics of an existing city of great age and character. An attitude of mind and an approach emerged. A route structure would be teased out of the existing grain of the city as if it were already there (echoes here of the ancient hedgerows, always stirring in the soil beneath Milton Keynes, which pop up to break the grid geometry). There would be no trampolining, no clowning with pop artefacts, no reaching for the synoptic vision and while there might be references these would be appropriately got up for the occasion.

An exploration of the texture of the city produced some structural clues:

The old drainage channels or singels, usually in grid formation, mirrors to the Dutch sky, bridges, grassy banks, avenues of poplars, pairs of straight roads.

Regular cross routes giving blocks about 240 x 50 metres or 15-20 frontages in length. At the conjunction of these linear elements a 'node' or focus of heightened activity.

The scale and consistency of the housing block as the definer of a primarily linear spatial framework.

It was first necessary to identify areas for retention. It was decided that housing at Katendrecht, between the disused docks, Rijnhaven and Maashaven, would be incorporated into the proposals, as would be the whole of Afrikaanderwijk and housing east of the railway at Feyenoord. These decisions created five separate development areas, two of them of substantial size, first the peninsula between Rijnhaven and Maashaven and second, the whole of the area incorporating Binnenhaven and Spoortweghaven, and three smaller areas, one an open square in the centre of Afrikaander-

3 Road structure.

4 Public open space.

5 Existing buildings retained.

6 Part axonometric.

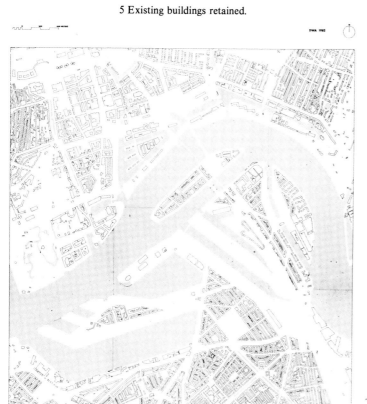

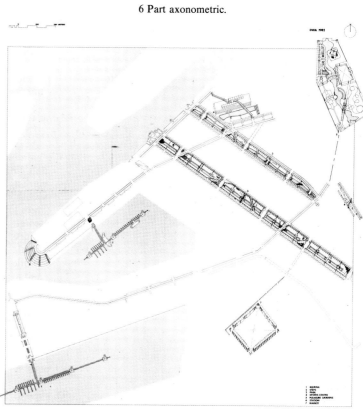

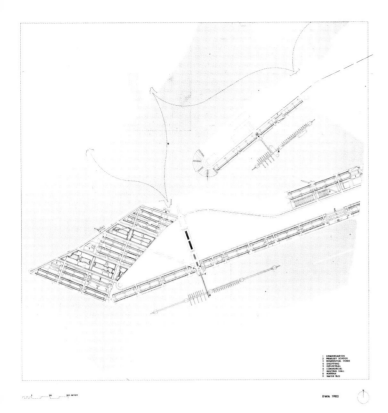

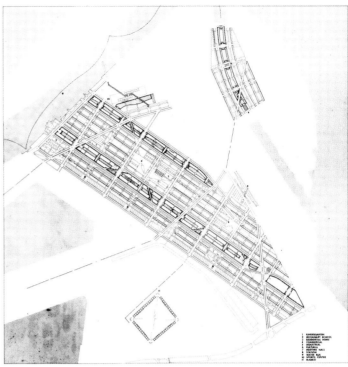

7 West section of site.

8 East section of site.

wijk. All of these areas except the latter had extensive water edges.

The broken characteristics of the area suggested that the route structure which would form the functional and spatial matrix for the proposals would need to have a number of complementary characteristics. It would need to be an extension of the existing structural frame of the city, a tensile force providing spatial continuity in scattered locations, a satisfactory interpretation of the city's formal texture and a basis for the design of a series of urban spaces giving the area a sense of unity and identity.

In the proposals each of these objectives is met by the overlay of levels in the route structure. At the primary level, three cross routes bridging Binnenhaven and Spoortweghaven extend existing main routes east and west from Katendrecht, Afrikaanderwijk and Feyenoord to provide a distributor frame and link the area to the city's existing route structure.

The role of the second level in the structure is to develop the city's characteristic grain by introducing the singel and cross route theme. This is done by using the exposed water and hard edges of the havens as the basis for linear promenades bridged by the primary and secondary cross routes. These promenades or avenues are the key to the character of the scheme – water, a polished perspective of light, shade under bridges, twin avenues of broad-leafed trees, gardens, hedges and two twin-lane roads. For reliable bearing conditions buildings are set back 15 metres from the existing water's edge so that there is a wide corridor of 120 metres and, for enclosure, the meter of four and five storey apartment buildings.

To complete the second level in the route structure cross routes are added and these give the rhythm of 240 x 50 metre blocks. These are

used for access to the courts and parking areas at the rear of the apartment buildings.

Finally the third layer in the route structure is added – a system of walkways and cycle routes. First there are footways parallel to and at the same spacing as the secondary road cross routes. These are covered ways which bridge the singles and form the principal points of entry for pedestrians to the apartment courts. So far it is a strictly orthogonal spatial matrix which is linear, horizontal, furnished with sky, trees, water. This is the replication of the texture of the city. Now, in the Binnenhaven/Spoortweghaven complex, the route grid is broken in order to focus the spatial energy of the the structure on the two most important and particular public spaces in the scheme. Diagonal routes are created linking the corners of the two quadrilaterals formed by the primary road linear and cross routes. At the conjunction of these diagonals are created, to the north, a public square with a hall, library and school and a link to the sports centre at the northern corner of the site, and to the south, a commercial square with shops, offices and a link to the new station. The network of routes at the third layer is rich with small corners, courts and enclosures and with the detailed particularities of urban life – paved surfaces, seats, children's play frames, flower stalls, shelters and awnings.

The form of the housing is complementary to the organisation of the route structure and there are also clear references, as a walk around the Woningboun area of Rotterdam and a review of the work of Ten Bosch, Otten, Oup, Brinkman and others will indicate. The four and five storey apartment blocks articulate both public and private space. At the front, the apartments look out over water, gardens, parks and promenades and present an elegant, modulated but low-key

public face. At the rear, the buildings enclose intimate hard surfaced courts containing parking and children's play areas and elevations are more complex and textured. At the end of the pairs of courts where primary and secondary cross routes break the linear blocks, activity is intensified at ground level with shops, bars and small commercial operations. At the private end of the courts, where pedestrian routes cross, there are community activities, laundries, playschools and local offices.

In the Rotterdam scheme the development of an urban geometry can be seen in which each level in the route structure has a role which is both reciprocal and independent – primary level: structural continuity; secondary level: textural consistency; tertiary level: complexity and particularity. Thus, in descending levels in the structure, we proceed from an emphasis on the ordering characteristics of the geometry to a process of fragmentation in which the potential of the structure for achieving variations and complexities is revealed. At every level, the role of the structure in ordering and unifying space is perceptible, even if as an echo or murmur and all spaces within the matrix are of equal status. There are no hierarchies.

The theme which persists in the development of Walker's work in urban structures is of course the quality of urban spaces within the route structure. Common to all uses for which the city exists is movement, and movement, which takes place in the armature of the city and in the spaces between buildings, is seen as the principal purpose of all urban structure. So the business of the city designer is to invent a spatial geometry which sustains the movement on which the life of the city depends, and provides the setting in which we may act out with dignity the ceremonies and dramas of urban life.

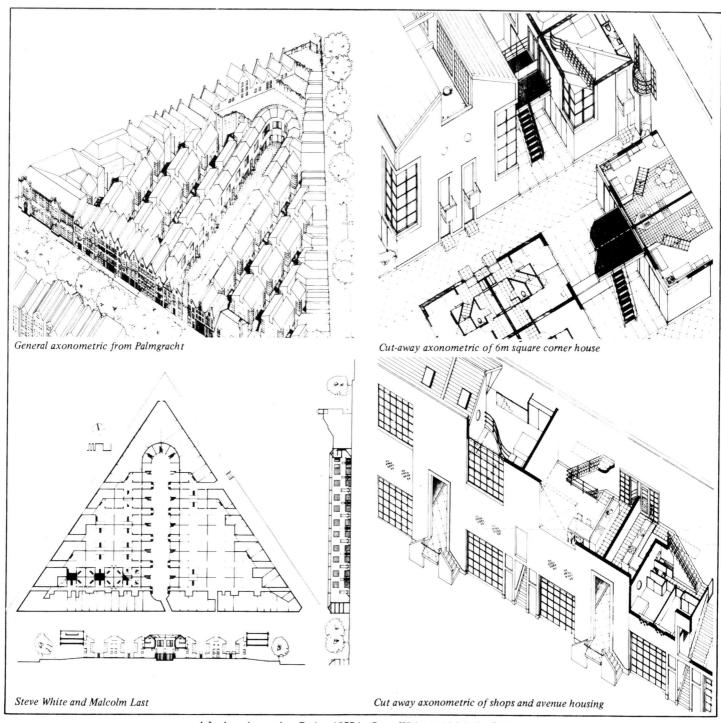

General axonometric from Palmgracht

Cut-away axonometric of 6m square corner house

Steve White and Malcolm Last

Cut away axonometric of shops and avenue housing

1 Jordaan Amsterdam Project 1977 by Steve White and Malcolm Last.

2 Urban Villas Project 1981 by Di Hope.

Christopher Cross

ROYAL COLLEGE OF ART STUDENT PROJECTS

The School of Environmental Design is one of the sixteen post-graduate art and design schools within the Royal College of Art. The thirty or so students are about equally contributed from architecture and design first degree backgrounds.

The School has, during the last ten years, developed a structured course integrating the study of Architecture, Landscape Design and Interior Design as a totality. The scope of the work undertaken ranges from the detailed design of interior space within an architectural context to the consideration of urban design projects. Work is valued that combines considerations at extremes of scale. Although personal programmes are developed and pursued, often in association with other departments in the College, students are generally encouraged to work to guidelines set by the staff to allow learning by comparison. The acquiring of the skill to draw effectively is particularly emphasised. The School attaches great importance to the thorough completion of work. This often results in the re-working and development of projects from early years in the final part of the course.

The academic programme is directed by John Miller, Professor since 1975, with a small nucleus of staff (all practising architects) and a wide range of visitors. This article reviews urban design work undertaken in the School during the last ten years, a period strongly influenced by Edward Jones, Senior Tutor until late 1982.

The Barcelona Project of 1977 typically summarises preoccupations of that time. The frustration and impotence of architects when faced with the full development of the modern city (for which of course they have hardly any responsibility) and a lingering megalomania from the last throes of the Modern Movement provoked a reappraisal of historic precedents. If the School has been criticised as over-influenced by European ideas, it is because these, and the work in the American East Coast schools, seemed more vital at the time and contrasted with the eclectic dabbling in other London schools. The writings of Colin Rowe were particularly respected – most of the staff have visited Cornell as lecturers and critics.

Leon Krier, who was responsible for the Barcelona Project with Edward Jones, wrote in

the programme – 'until its transformation in the nineteenth century and destruction in the twentieth century, the urban block was the key element of any socially and physically cohesive urban pattern of streets and squares, of monuments and urban fabric. If the European city is to be saved, it must be recomposed from urban techniques to be learnt from the history of the city.' Students designed within a fine grid superimposed on Cerda's grid of the nineteenth century. The urban avenues of this spatial megastructure were seen as still retaining validity as a technical and visual instrument to organise a large metropolitan body.

In contrast to the prevailing circumstances in which armies of specialists might surround themselves with data and labour for years to organise the typical chaos of a modern city (or hospital) it seemed that there should be a return to the use of traditional systems and paradigms. With a rediscovered understanding of these systems it might be quickly possible to propose new cities or, more believably, interventions within older cities. Whereas in our recent tradition architects have allowed themselves to be dis-

3,4 Kensington Project 1979 by Chris Hay.

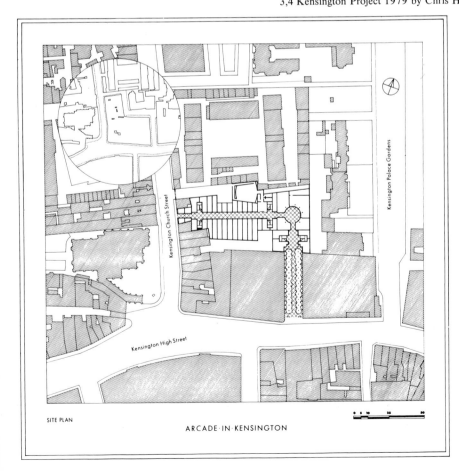

SITE PLAN

ARCADE·IN·KENSINGTON

INTERIOR

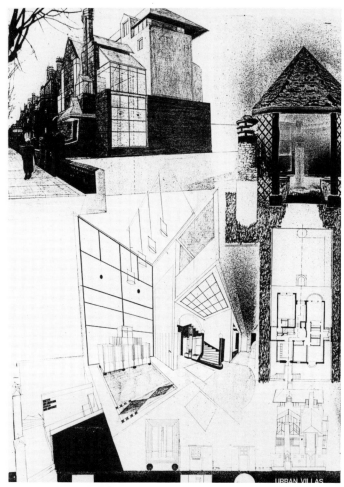

5 Urban Villas Project 1981 by Ken Armstrong.

6 Hotel Particuliere Project 1981 by Ed Bonness.

tracted by pre-architectural circumstances which seem to have absorbed all their energy leaving visually and spatially primitive buildings almost as an afterthought, this new understanding should allow undistracted concentration on buildings and their details.

The arcade, street, court and city block were regular preoccupations in School projects that supported a definite point of view about the consolidation of what is left of the traditional city. The Bond Street Arcade Project of 1976 (Kenneth Frampton and Edward Jones) and the Kensington Project of 1978 (Elia Zhengelis) sought to examine mechanisms of the traditional city that might be reinterpreted. The arcade was a vehicle to remind students of the need to rediscover the potency of the enclosed void as against the free-standing solid so eloquently expounded by Colin Rowe. From the Bond Street programme: 'Of all the building types thrown up by the nineteenth century, the arcade or gallery still proffers itself as a type for the reintegration of the existing urban fabric. Originating in the spontaneous consolidation of shopping streets in the first two decades of the last century, the arcade along with the conservatory, the market hall and the railway terminus, arose as an encapsulating device by which to establish the city in miniature. The arcade, like the oriental bazaar, was invariably conceived as a parasitical structure whose facade was entirely internal, an ambiguous element which, facing onto a glazed street, was both an inside and an outside at the same time.'

The revaluing of old systems led to a series of survey projects. Historical surveys that traced the evolution of urban areas tried to divine underlying systems that might be respected or extended in new projects. Other projects required traditional measured drawings of building. In his book with Christopher Woodward, *The Architecture of London*, Edward Jones included a survey of squares carried out by RCA students. A graphic survey of context and precedent has now become the preliminary to most design work. Whereas most projects have been deliberately set within the area of immediate experience of staff and students – Victorian Inner London – in contrast, in the Jordaan Amsterdam Project of 1977 run in association with schools in Delft and Düsseldorf, students considered the possibilities for the re-use of old warehouse buildings on a triangular site bounded on two sides by canals. New pieces could be inserted in the centre of the block within the matrix of old alleys that connected the site back to the centre of the city.

By the late 1970s, with the gathering depression and consequent unlikelihood of major public building projects, let alone large scale site clearance in the centre of London, we became critical of working at an over-ambitious scale. The Metal Exchange Project of 1980 (Christopher Cross) examined ways of building to support the tight medieval network of the traditional business 'City'. It was intended to offer a critique of the gratuitous destruction of the area by business architects which continues

almost unquestioned. It sought to demonstrate that careful infill at small scale could complement the old system without compromising artistic integrity – urban dentistry. Students pursued the same theme in the 1981 RIBA Student 'Corner' Project (Ted Cullinan). A number were premiated.

Within the distinction of monument and fabric, the fabric of Inner London is generally the network of rows of terrace houses. Various programmes have examined ways of working within or extending this system. Although sites exist, for example in Docklands, it is difficult to imagine satisfactory new terraces being built at anything like the scale of, say, Kensington. Endless rows of two or three-storey terraces are a dismal prospect. Sites in the areas of transition between the inner city and its suburban fringe where there is still a sense of urban scale have been studied for clues. The Urban Villas Project of 1981 (Edward Jones and Jeremy Dixon) sought to examine an appropriate new urban building block for a site in Swiss Cottage based on the surrounding late Victorian System of giant semi-detached villas. While the old buildings have become sub-divided over time, the new were to be built as apartments but retain references to the hierarchical order of a single large house while allowing the street to read as a continuous system of buildings. The villas as free-standing solids were contrasted to the unbuilt voids of the Paris courts in the Hotel Particuliere Project (Fernando Montes). Schemes were developed in parallel with

HOLLAND PARK
TRANSFORMATION OF THE GARDENS

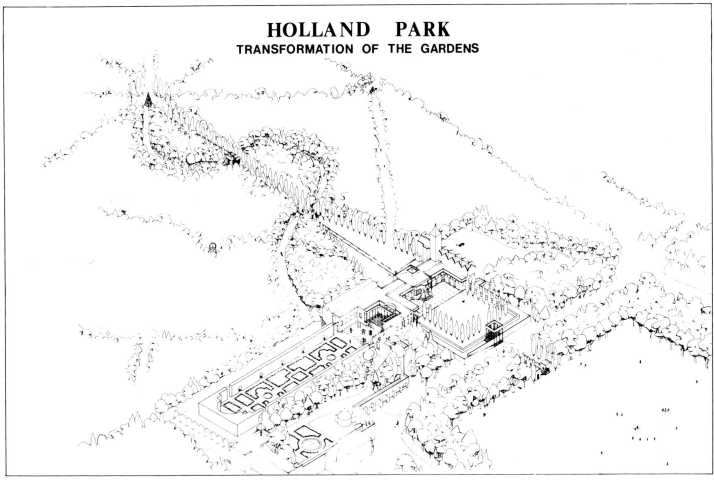

7 Holland Park Project 1979 by Graham Fairly.

students in Paris leading to a joint criticism of work and an exhibition.

If life in the main city streets has become diminished by the noise and dirt of traffic and the upkeep of large structures has become an increasing strain, life in the backland and mews areas has become increasingly attractive. A number of projects, particularly for housing in Camden Mews 1979 (Su Rogers), have examined the internal landscape of the mews and studio house.

There are obvious parallels between the urban and landscape evolution, a theme frequently pursued in the School. In the survey of Stowe of 1978 (Edward Jones and Su Rogers), the displacement of the French system of axis and formal avenues by the English contrived

'natural' arrangement is clearly shown. The School's enjoyment of French influence is demonstrated in projects such as the Transformation of the Gardens at Holland Park, 1979 and the Glasgow Green project of 1980. The Greenwich Project of 1981 (Su Rogers) explored the possibilities of extending the main axis of the park through the Royal Hospital and across the Thames into the areas of derelict dockland.

The preoccupation with ideal systems might be seen as a striving for security and seems in retrospect somewhat naive and evasive. Most work, although developed to a high standard, remained schematic. While an understanding of the underlying structure of the city is a valuable asset, the uncomfortable lesson of the regular

experience of Central London is to be faced with the quality of its quite ordinary buildings.

In a recent project intended as a critique of the National Gallery Extension Competition, students found the greatest difficulty in devising any architectural proposition that could stand with Wilkin's relatively lowly regarded building. If the period in which we re-learnt the principles of city organisation and became preoccupied by types and models is now past, the immediate task would seem to be to return to the artistic issues of architecture. To develop skill and visual sophistication in the making of buildings at perhaps quite a modest scale. With James Gowan as Senior Tutor, this academic year has begun with a reappraisal of Bedford Park and the English Arts and Craft Movement.

8 Survey of Stowe, 1978.

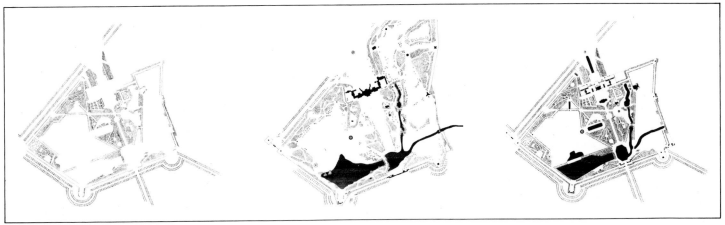

O M Ungers
KULTURFORUM, BERLIN

The area at Kemperplatz, which was given the ambitious name 'Kulturforum', presents itself today as just a fragmentary and almost co-incidental urban district despite the eminent buildings erected after World War II. It is impossible to speak here of a meaningful urban context and one wonders what has happened to this urban area, formerly so important, during the many years of rebuilding after the war. The fatally wrong first decision leading to this situation was the total denial of the area's history by planners and other responsible people, a denial that amounted to a negation and almost a complete destruction of this historically valid urban area. Naive visionaries, ambitious utopians and unhesitant traffic-engineers were involved in this decision as well as politicians trying to do their best. Some people believed in an 'Arcadia' in the heart of Berlin, and had in mind an urban landscape with the sacred places of culture: they wanted a forum of the spirit, the dream of pilgrim areas of culture nestling among the Garden of Eden, to be realised there. Others, the tough realists, believed in the 'verkehrsgerechte Stadt' (traffic-expedient city) with expressways and con-trolled crossroads. Yet no-one concerned with planning, design and development wanted to have anything to do with the history of the square. Nor did anybody recognise the hidden possibilities in taking up tradition. Tradition

was eliminated and its remaining traces after the war covered over.

What we experience today is an area without history, a square without tradition and, although newly built, without connection. It represents nothing more than a coincidence, a coincidence of decisions and the mechanisms of general judgements. Notions, and above all emotions and feelings of resentment, determine the place where rational meaningful urbanity would have been appropriate.

If one wants to look at what came from vastly different lobbies not only negatively but as a representation of a positive creative process, one can best describe this area as a dialectical urban field, a field of culture on which thesis and antithesis are set in opposition to each other. To put this assessment negatively, one could also say that here in the surroundings of Kemper-platz, the so-called 'Kulturforum' at the edge of the Tiergarten, an area has been created where one building simply stands next to another: thesis beside thesis, object beside object, one thing beside another: just like stones lying beside each other, having no relationship, and to a certain extent bereft of content.

What we have here is probably nothing but an accumulation of giants: an assemblage of various architectures, a twentieth-century talent show. This, it seems, is not only the meaning but also the appearance of this peculiar

area which had been conceived, planned and desired as a 'culture band' along the river Spree.

What remains to be done, now that the main things have already happened? It remains to supplement, to complete and, above all, to realise visible spatial orders in a relatively unordered chaos. The restlessness of forms, spaces and buildings can only be met with restraint and the clarity and simplicity of architectonic forms. After all, the big buildings are already built and thus the main act is over: the issue now is the epilogue, the background matters, and it is important, where possible, to capture those urban spaces which have been lost to self-sufficient architecture and to make them visible, even as fragments. The task now is to design urban spaces like squares and streets with unambiguous borders and demarcations.

The Kemperplatz itself can no longer be just a literary creation describing an area which does not exist in reality except on a street sign and which therefore has no meaning for a visitor. A square should allow for physical experience: it needs clear borders and walls and unambiguous contours, both in order to con-stitute the space of the square and to intensify this experience. This is the characteristic which distinguishes the urban square from the village green: the urban square is clear, bordered, readable, distinct, and strictly geometrical,

1 Site plan of the existing area.

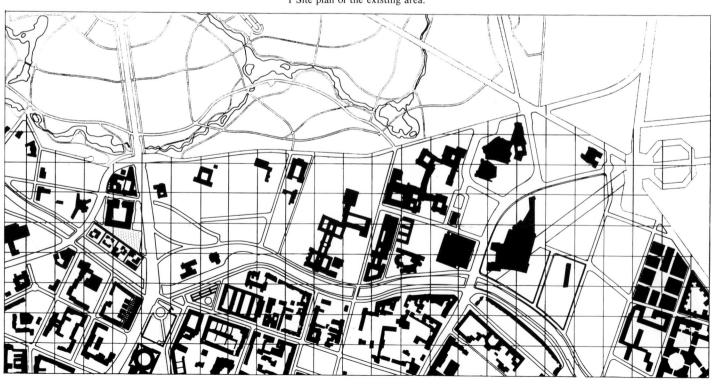

whereas the village green has fluid contours and is simply an enlargement of a space which cannot be defined. Yet here in the cultural centre of Berlin it is not the village green, the idyll of the accidental, which is appropriate but the ordering and urban strictness of a central square with walls and an urban, not a suburban or rural, atmosphere. Only an unambiguously defined urban space will join the freely developing pieces of architecture scattered around in a meaningful spatial connection. This is the reason why the geometry of the square is related to the rational geometry of the National Gallery and not to that of the confusing and not very comprehensible forms of the other buildings. The Matthäikirchplatz should be the centre and, given its urban importance, should become the actual fixed point, the support for the whole Kulturforum, like an anchor which is dropped in order to calm the restless and rotating volumes.

Besides the many already existing and planned buildings or those currently under construction, what remains to complete the building catalogue is the construction of a tower building: a building form which should not be missing in a complex ensemble, especially since an observation tower could provide a bird's-eye view of the urban image. One has to admit that the heterogenous image of the Kulturforum at the Kemperplatz is better comprehended from above than from the perspective of the pedestrian; many things which cannot be understood while looking at them from below become coherent and make sense once they are seen from an aerial perspective. Because the historical facades of streets and squares have been given up, a tower building seems to be the only solution, enriching one's experience by a view of the roof facades and the horizontal surfaces of the buildings. Any forum without a tower building is like a house without a roof.

The Kulturforum at Kemperplatz needs such a building to be rounded off and completed, a 'campanile' or a distinct symbol which can be seen from afar.

Apart from tower and square, two other missing urban elements will be inserted into the Kulturforum situation: the street and the park. Up until now, the persecuting ideology of transposing a countryside atmosphere into an urban context has so far left no place for such elements. One can presume that they were negated for ideological reasons, thus reducing the street to a street band and the park to an open landscape. Even despite the fact that Potsdamer Strasse, a boulevard of historical significance, cannot be re-established because the Staatbibliothek obstructs its original route, a new parallel street space should be created which, although just a fragment, would call to mind the former urban configuration. The completion of this space would be constituted by the urban park behind the buildings running along the street. The connection of park and dwelling is not only a formal one: the two functions of dwelling and relaxation, or residence and leisure, should connect both in terms of space as well as design. These two paramount areas should be unified in an urban expression (distinct from the idea of landscape) and thus contribute to and reformulate the urban character of the district.

Finally, the two areas at the eastern and western edges of the Kulturforum should also be mentioned. The first is the area of the former Potsdam railway station and the second the so-called Bendlerblock. If one is to build on these areas, which would be worthwhile, then one should definitely think of housing so that at least the border areas of the Kulturforum get some activity: this urban district would otherwise remain deserted. From a city planning point of view, these areas are two large open fields on each of which habitation could be introduced by two prototypical forms. The first area, the former Potsdam railway station, calls for the revitalisation of a dwelling type originating in England with the idea of a garden city. This type then very quickly spread to the Continent and succeeded as a humane alternative to the inhumane living conditions in the big cities; in Berlin it was first of all to be found in the Westend, then in Lichterfelde and later in Zehlendorf. Accordingly, the terms 'living in the green', urban villa and urban garden describe a form of dwelling which is also typical of Berlin and which should be brought into connection with the idea of the Forum. The other form of dwelling stems originally from Berlin and relates to the proposals for ribbon or linear building development in Berlin-Haselhorst as well as to many other examples which were typical of urban development during the 1920s and are still a convincing solution. This is also the kind of development which inspired Hilberseimer's extreme concept for rebuilding Berlin. Especially in this city, the issue of ribbon development has gone through many variations; and as we are dealing here with a Forum, the best and most beautiful should be brought together, including ribbon development in its strict and consistent form.

Taken all together (the existing buildings; the ones which are under construction; the planned and newly proposed buildings, Kemperplatz; the Matthäikirchplatz with the angled parish house; the new street substituting for the older Potsdamer Strasse with its bordering buildings and the two corners; the urban parks; the tower building on a pedestal like the National Gallery; the garden city in the east and the linear ribbon city in the west including the Bendlerblock; the fragments; the Hotel Esplanade; the wonderful church by Stühler, the only building which survived the

2 New site plan of the area.

57

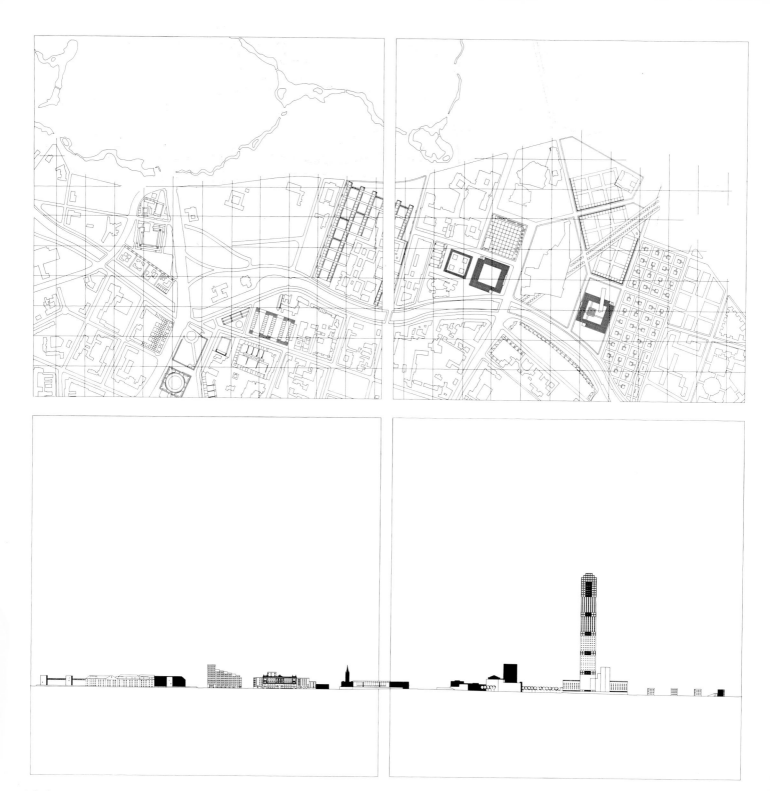

tabula rasa campaign; the National Gallery; the German Forschungsgesellschaft (Research Society) which became a little bit too small and the museums 'Preussischer Kulturbesitz' which came out far too big; the State Library and the already legendary Philharmonic) all these elements of the Forum – the differences, the contradictions, the discontinuities – are to be summaried under the pretentious title 'Kulturforum'. This can only mean a garden, a square on which all kinds of architectural culture, including contradictory ones, have their place. What else can be meant by Kulturforum? Certainly not uniformity, a horrible attempt to make everything alike. The city, and especially the forum of a city, unlike the village lives from contradictions and not from uniformity. And if the issue here in the Landwehrkanal area of Berlin is to create anew what has been lost in another area with the Museumsinsel, then this cannot mean the spirit of the village or the provincialism of adaptation; rather urbanity, represented through the variety of contradictions and dialectical differences, should determine the area. If this chance is missed again, one will have to realise one day that the chance to create urbanity, rather than a village atmosphere, has been gambled away for a second time. Resentments do not help. The respect for the area's history, missing for so long, now demands a break from uniformity and the narrow, one-sided interpretations of objects and forms.

This area has to liberate itself from almost unbearable pressures in order to release the 'other', the opposite, something going beyond its present scope. The existing buildings would not be appreciated less by this release, for it is in acknowledging differences that true respect lies. The opportunity has arisen to seek an alternative, to manifest it and ignore barriers, not out of protest and polemicism but out of respect for the new and latest history of the area.

Translated from the German by Romana Schneider

3 Site plan of the entire urban space between Askanischem Platz and Lützowplatz.

4 Elevation showing the general aspect of the town near the Landwehrkanal. The prospect shows the stringing of individual buildings along the Landwehrkanal like pearls on a necklace, thus emphasising the significance of the Landwehrkanal as an attractive as well as valuable inner-city waterway.

5,6 Axonometric of the 'Kulturforum Berlin' planning area. In the centre of the district is the Matthaikirchplatz with the Stuhlkirche (church), where an angle-form building is constructed. The plaza and building reiterate the geometry of the National Gallery, and the latter building expands from west to east into a square courtyard. In the eastern part a tower building stands on a platform

similar to the podium construction of the National Gallery. Potsdamer Strasse remains as a fragment, and this historical vestige is preserved. The new Potsdamer Strasse is determined by two angled corner buildings, the inner zone of each enclosing public areas. In the eastern part of the district near the Potsdam Railway Station is a space of city houses paralleling another site in the western area.

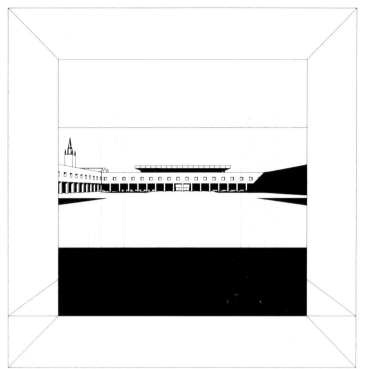

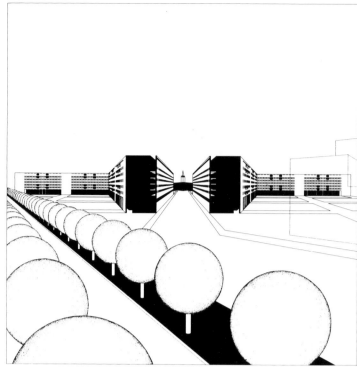

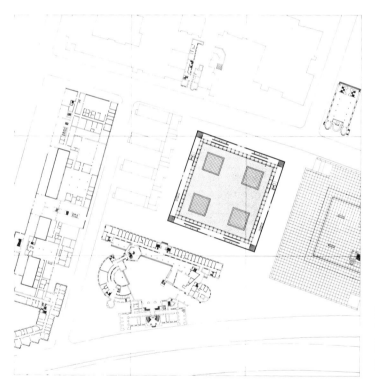

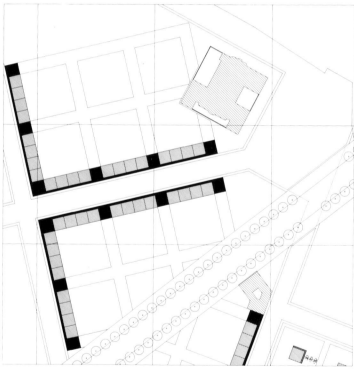

7 Extension of the National Gallery, perspective. The National Gallery expands into a sculpture courtyard enclosed by a two-storey building. The gallery rooms are grouped on the ground floor around four courtwells. The overhead building is a circulating gallery corridor leading to administration and service rooms.

8 Cross-section of the Museum Garden ground floor.

9 Living Area Housing on Potsdamer Strasse with a view of the Matthaikirche Steeple, perspective. The housing on Potsdamer Strasse develops from two angle-form partitions or walls. In each building a gallery corridor faces the street, while the rest of the building faces a self-contained inner park. The living space – divided into floors and maisonettes – is accessible by means of the outside corridor. On the ground floor are social and service rooms.

10 Site plan of angle-plan buildings and street layout.

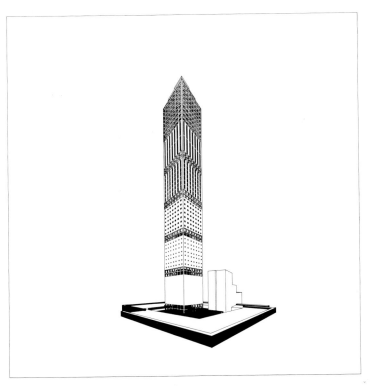

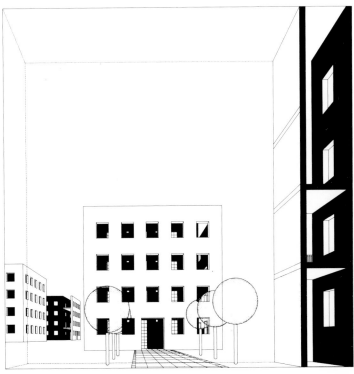

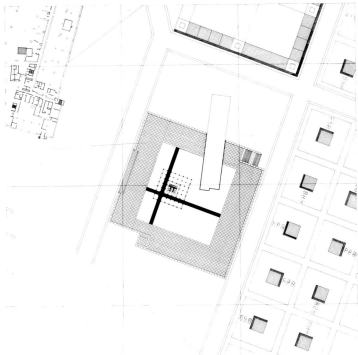

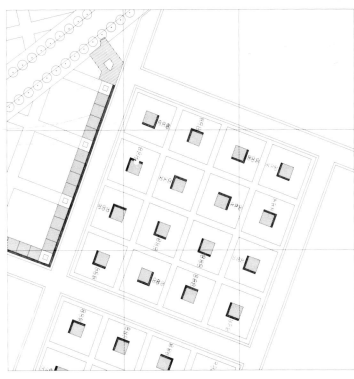

11 Skyscraper at Landwehrkanal, perspective. The skyscraper is typologically conceived of as a tower which rises from a platform base similar to the National Gallery. Five viewing plateaux, one every eight floors, permit an overview of the city from different heights. The top of the tower is a glass-enclosed city museum. The tower develops over five functional sections. In the first section are special rooms, in the next one above is a hotel, above that are residences, then offices, and in the last section is the Institute. The existing hotel is the integral foundation of the complex. At night the tapering point of the tower is lit as a landmark.
12 Site plan.

13 Rented housing in the former Potsdam Railway Station area, perspective. The buildings of the former Potsdam Railway Station become converted into housing with a uniform distribution network. The houses are four-storey and contain either four dwellings or two maisonettes. The openings to the individual residences are approached from an outward-looking staircase which is angle-formed over two sides of the building. In the stairwell area are also balconies, residual rooms and entry spaces. Each garden can be freely shaped in front of the entrances.
14 Site plan.

Richard Rogers & Partners

PROPOSAL FOR THE BANKS OF THE RIVER ARNO, FLORENCE

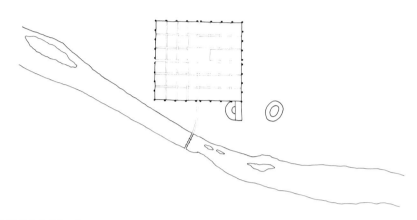

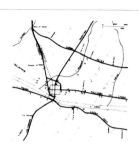

Florence became a Roman colony (Florentia) around 60 AD for strategic and territorial reasons. The urban map of the Roman period is a square of perpendicular streets forming a series of islands or blocks 60 x 70m and orientated on north-south and east-west axes legible even in the existing Via Roma (Vardo) and Via Strozzi (Decumano), at the intersection of which was the Forum (Piazza della Repubblica).

Public works were built, such as towers, aqueducts, kilns, wells and fountains, and the paving of streets; across the Arno, then navigable up to the mouth of the river, the first masonry bridge was built to allow the connection of territory with the Via Cassia.

Slightly beyond the bridge was the harbour; essentially a timber wharf, it would achieve greater function and importance in the medieval period for the transport of spices, wool, minerals and construction materials.

THE ROMAN CITY

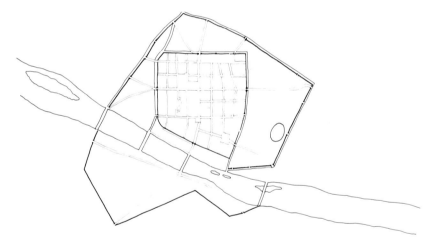

Medieval Florence expanded on both banks of the Arno, making the construction of new connections between shores necessary (Ponte alla Carraia, 1220; Ponte alle Grazie, 1237; Ponte S Trinita, 1252), and for defensive reasons masonry walls like pliers were built on the river with fortified banks to close off the interior from either the mountain or the valley.

The Arno still constituted the key point of reference for city life: its water generated the hydraulic power for the grain mills, and served wool weaving factories, dye-works, tanners, cloth manufacturers. Located along its banks were support industries, open courts, shops and the highest density of housing in the city. The river hosted shows and festivals when the 'fiorentini' would converge on its banks and bridges to enjoy and further animate the spectacle.

THE MEDIEVAL CITY

1 The Roman and medieval city.

3-6 Florence in 1744,

Richard Rogers and Partners with Claudio Cantella (design team Claudio Cantella, Philip Gumuchdjian, Marco Goldschmied, Gennaro Picardi, Richard Rogers, Alan Stanton, John Young).
Hydraulic Engineer Enrico Bougleux.

Photographs by G Picardi and E Squilloni.

Brief
To establish a new pedestrian realm for residents and visitors, restore the neglected river banks of the Arno and bring back life to the river.

Design Analysis
Traditionally, Florence's Arno enriched the life of the city and was the focus for bustling activity – walking, fishing, river pageant, theatre, sailing and merchant transport. Until recent times the streets along the river banks facilitated and enforced these diverse activities.

Since the advent of the motorcar, these same riverside streets have become heavily congested and now form a continuous collar of traffic cutting off the river. The pedestrians that walk on the narrow, crowded and often unsafe pavements are dissuaded from lingering because of noise, fumes and tall balustrades – raised against flooding. The Arno has, as a result, fallen into disuse; its banks, collecting rubble, silt and urban waste are the witness of the declining role of the river as a public resource.

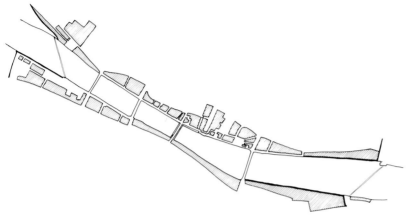

THE RENAISSANCE CITY

Since the 1400s there was an intense development of building programmes with the progressive saturation of the areas still open within the city walls and the creation of a few tracts of paths along the Arno (*lungarni*).

Additionally, the weirs of S Niccolo (S Michele) and S Rosa were built to improve the efficiency of the mills and to regulate the level and flow of the river through the centre of the city.

In the 1500s, at first with Baldassarre Peruzzi and then with Michelangelo from 1529, an improvement of the fortification system was accomplished (as a defense against the use of artillery) and also an improvement of the river's hydraulic system. These related projects were elaborated within a Civic Department of Engineering, where, amongst others, Ammannati and Buontalenti worked.

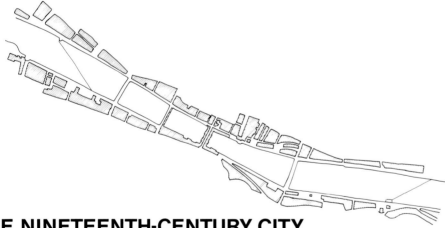

THE NINETEENTH-CENTURY CITY

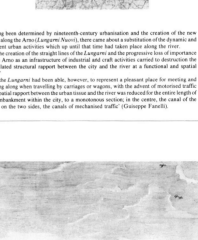

Having been determined by nineteenth-century urbanisation and the creation of the new paths along the Arno (*Lungarni Nuovi*), there came about a substitution of the dynamic and different urban activities which up until that time had taken place along the river.

'The creation of the straight lines of the *Lungarni* and the progressive loss of importance of the Arno as an infrastructure of industrial and craft activities carried to destruction the articulated structural rapport between the city and the river at a functional and spatial level.'

If the *Lungarni* had been able, however, to represent a pleasant place for meeting and moving along when travelling by carriages or wagons, with the advent of motorised traffic the 'spatial rapport between the urban tissue and the river was reduced for the entire length of the embankment within the city, to a monotonous section; in the centre, the canal of the river; on the two sides, the canals of mechanised traffic' (Guiseppe Fanelli).

engravings by Zocchi.

2 The Renaissance and nineteenth-century city.

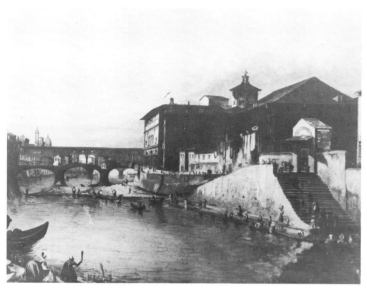

7-9 The image of the quay yesterday (nineteenth-century painting by Moricci), today and tomorrow.

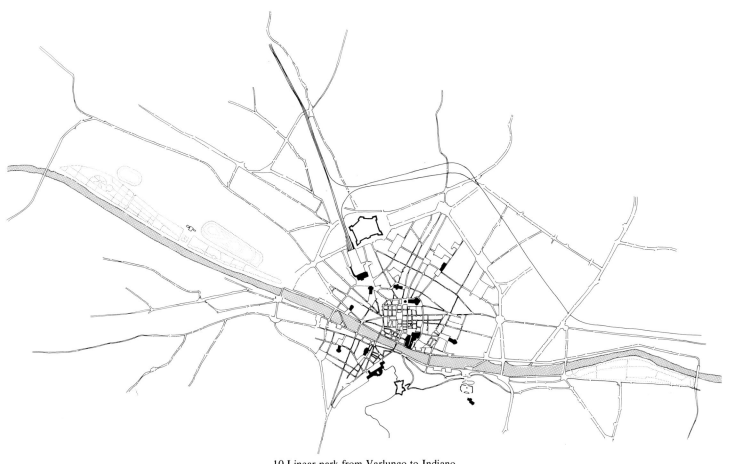

10 Linear park from Varlungo to Indiano.

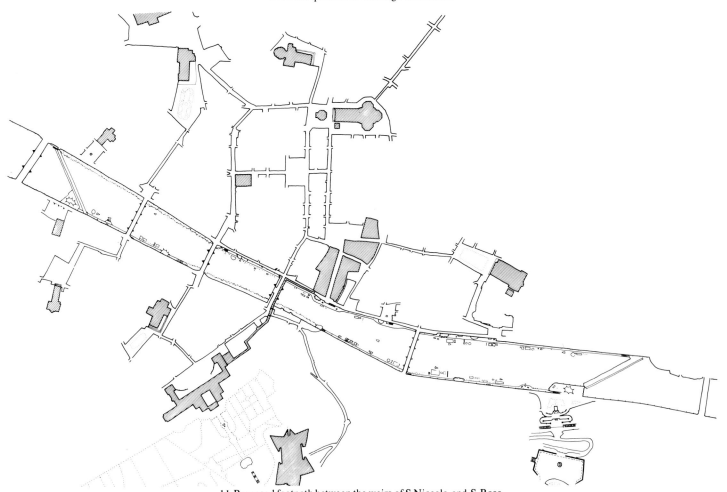

11 Proposed footpath between the weirs of S Niccolo and S Rosa.

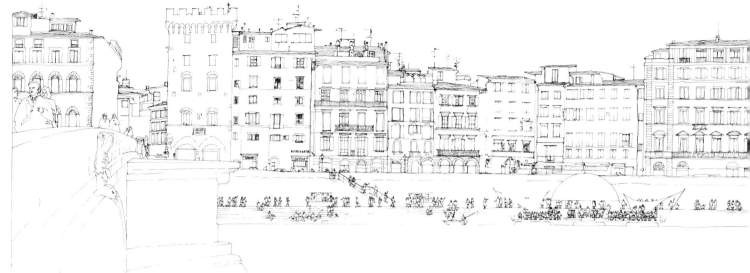

Il Percorso da S.Trinita a Ponte Vecchio in Sponda Destra

Design

The project proposes the creation of a linear park along the banks of the river, stretching from city centre to suburbs: a framework woven into the existing pedestrian network of the city within which activities of all kinds would be encouraged and promoted: a lung for an over-crowded city.

The new walk offers the pedestrian (be he casual user, the tourist, the suburban commuter) a safe, relaxing and pleasant walk along the river – opening new and forgotten views of the city and its historic buildings.

The 'percorso attrezzato' (serviced route) itself would, particularly during the summer months, become a dynamic artery with stalls, cafés, bars, restaurants, information services and entertainment facilities cut into the banks or floating on rafts, enlivening the river with tents, canopies, banners and sunshades – the whole encouraging the use of the Arno and providing the opportunity for leisure without stress or risk.

The path would extend for five miles between the suburbs of Varlungo and Indiano, connecting two large existing parks. Special

12 The route between S Trinita

13 Below the Ponte Vecchio.

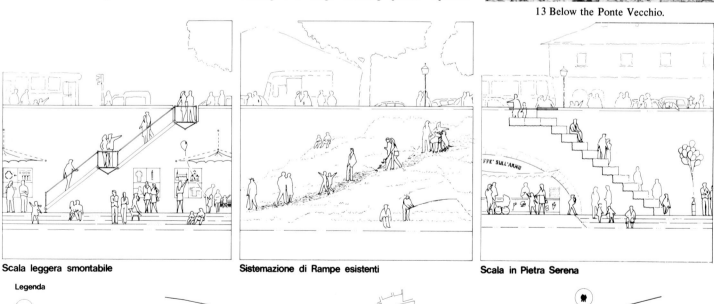

Scala leggera smontabile   Sistemazione di Rampe esistenti   Scala in Pietra Serena

Legenda

- 👥   Accessi Pedonali
- ↘   ''   Mezzo di Manutenzione
- ▲   ''   Esistenti / da consolidare
- △   ''   Proposti
- ——   Il Percorso

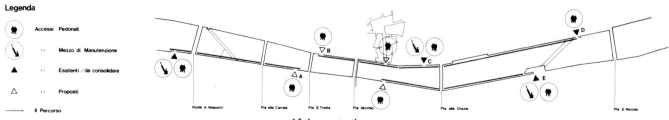

15 Access to the route.

and Ponte Vecchio.

14 Danger on the Lungarno.

attention has been given to the central section where the design utilises and consolidates existing paths passing between major monuments and historic bridges: the Ponte Vecchio, the only bridge in Florence to survive the German Second World War bombing; and the Santa Trinita, reconstructed after the war to the original Ammannati design of 1577 (after Michelangelo's drawings).

Calculating from data for the period 1968-82, it was established that a level of 43 metres above sea level remains unaffected by flooding for at least eight months a year. In 1980-1981-1982, for example, there were only 49, 37, and 20 days respectively when a path at this level would have been submerged. Existing steps and ramps down to the water's edge would be restored and supplemented by lightweight steps and ramps, providing access for pedestrians, service and maintenance vehicles. The regularisation of the river banks and the establishment of an active management will improve the flow of the water and strengthen and encourage the existing flora and fauna.

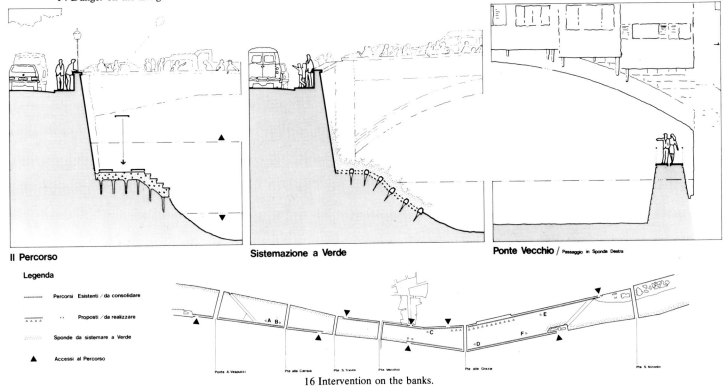

Il Percorso

Sistemazione a Verde

Ponte Vecchio / Passaggio in Sponda Destra

Legenda

— — —   Percorsi Esistenti / da consolidare

△ △ △ △   ''   Proposti / da realizzare

∴∴∴∴   Sponde da sistemare a Verde

▲   Accessi al Percorso

Ponte A.Vespucci   Pte alla Carraia   Pte S.Trinita   Pte Vecchio   Pte alle Grazie   Pte S.Niccolo

16 Intervention on the banks.

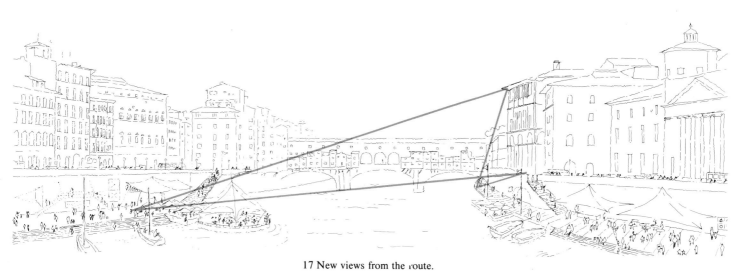

17 New views from the route.

18 Optimal level of the route and chart of accessibility.

1968 - 1982
Quando l'Arno ha superato Quota 43

Mesi piu' sfavorevoli degli ultimi 15 Anni *

Gennaio	1979	
Febbraio	'78	
Marzo	'74	
Aprile	'78	
Maggio	'82	
Giugno	68-82	
Luglio	''	
Agosto	''	
Settembre	'73	
Ottobre	'81	
Novembre	'80	
Dicembre	'81	

Giorni del Mese   0   5   10   15   20   25   30

* Dai dati dei Livelli di Piena registrati all'idrometro degli Uffizi e rielaborati

43

42.00   43.00   44.20
S.Rosa   Uffizi   S. Niccolo'

Quote del Percorso / Pendenza dell'1%

1980
316 Giorni Percorribili
49 '' Inagibili *

1981
328 Giorni Percorribili
37 '' Inagibili *

1982
345 Giorni Percorribili
20 '' Inagibili *

THE BATTLE FOR CORNER PROPERTIES IN BRUSSELS

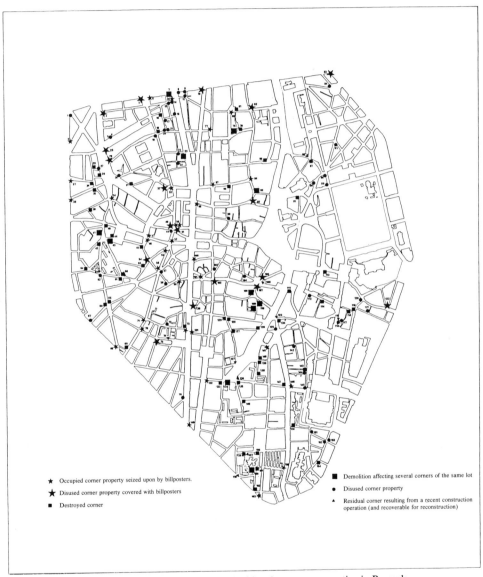

★ Occupied corner property seized upon by billposters.

★ Disused corner property covered with billposters

■ Destroyed corner

■ Demolition affecting several corners of the same lot

● Disused corner property

▲ Residual corner resulting from a recent construction operation (and recoverable for reconstruction)

1 Site plan showing types of dilapidated corner properties in Brussels.

A survey and four projects worked out in 1983 at the Archives d'Architecture Moderne by Annick Brauman, Maurice Culot, Alain Desmytter, Jean-Pierre Majot and Caroline Mierop for the bureau d'Urbanisme de l'Agglomeration of Brussels.

One can say that the good or bad health of a town is measured by the state of preservation of its corners.

Up to the thirties the angled plot had always been considered as choice building terrain sought after for private mansions, large luxury stores and then for panoramic apartment blocks.

After the war, architects and public powers neglected the treatment of corners which are now systematically denied or destroyed. This situation imperils the fundamental cohesion of the traditional urban structure and visually amplifies the city's state of aesthetic degradation: in effect, the impact of a destroyed corner goes far beyond that of the simple area that it occupies in the sun.

This is one of the reasons that the centre of present-day Brussels has an aspect of slum development unmatched in any other European capital.

The map charted by the Archives d'Architecture Moderne discovered not less than 163 cases of drifted corners (destroyed corners, abandoned properties or those surrendered to publicity . . .) within the perimeter of Brussel's historic centre. And this map itself is not exhaustive; it is intended to be a speech for the defence so that the political priority of renovation and reconstruction of corner properties may be redeemed.

Such operations would be easy to carry out and would stimulate the renovation of entire districts and would resurrect the city's image and identity.

By way of example, the Archives d'Architecture Moderne have realised four projects of reconstruction for destroyed corners in the centre of Brussels; these projects demonstrate that investments and land politics can be re-orientated towards the repair of the city.

2 Proposal.
3 Existing situation.

Project I

A destroyed corner on one of the grand 'Haussmanian' boulevards of the nineteenth century.

The project illustrates the repair of one of the busiest corner fragments of the Boulevard Anspach: the entrance to the underground is adjacent to the big store 'Les Galeries Anspach', at the corner of the Rue de l'Evêque.

The corner building which used to occupy this piece of land was destroyed during the construction work on the underground entrance and replaced by a side lift which disfigures the monumental perspective of the boulevard. The

footbridge which joins to the lateral street accentuates the visual impact of this destruction.

The new corner property which faithfully restores the boulevard's architectural characteristics re-establishes the unitary aspect of its monumental alignment.

On the ground floor the new property integrates the entrance to the underground, a newspaper kiosk and access to the department store; the storeys are assigned to the extensions of the store's commercial surfaces or to an independent programme of four levels of accommodation.

4 Proposal.

Project II

A small vague plot in a working-class and industrial district of the centre city.

This case is typical: a corner building is knocked down, is not reconstructed, and in a short time the site is invaded by the accessories of urban misery (signposts, public dustbins, parking lots, billboards . . .) which confirm its status as diminished wasted space.

This corner plot, situated in a very densely built district, is favourable for the construction of a small public space. This project recaptures the principles of simple and economical fittings, elaborated by the urban engineers of the nineteenth century, which constitute so many obstacles to degradation: an architectured garden enclosed by an iron gate, a pavement enlarged with two benches, two trees, streetlamps and a telephone box.

6 View of the site of the Old Palais de Justice.

7 Proposal.   8 Existing situation.

Project III
La Place de la Justice.

The great construction works of the railway and highway infrastructures undertaken during the 1950s and 60s in the very heart of Brussels have ripped open and completely disfigured the ancient Town Hall area, thus accentuating the piece cut out between the upper and lower part of the city: two shapeless spaces, one a part of a useless bridge road, a great vague terrain on one of the four corners of the site, traffic islands, entrances to underground parking lots, automobiles above, trains below. . . rarely pedestrians.

The project reconstitutes a true urban place which re-articulates the string of urban public spaces connecting the scale of the city, from the Sablons towards the Place Saint-Jean and then the Grand'Place.

The bridge road is done away with to build an intersection of level road systems and large pavements with staircases.

A mixed-use building (commercial and residential) is built on the vague area left on one of the corners of the site. A public edifice, containing a library and a large cafe, occupies the centre of the site and recalls by its classical composition, the ancient peristyle of the Palais de Justice which used to be situated approximately in this area. The project is completed by different secondary fittings: the creation of new entrances for the existing underground parking, enlargement of the pavements, the planting of trees, the erection of a new statue, street-lamps . . .

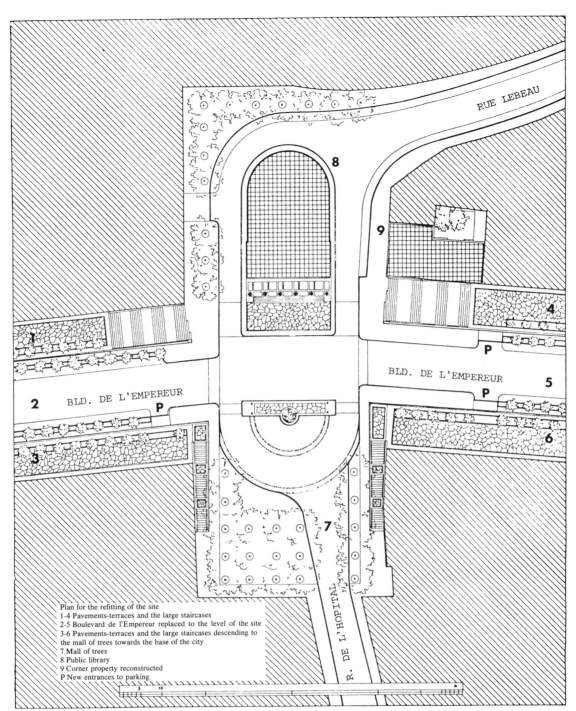

RUE LEBEAU

8

9

4

BLD. DE L'EMPEREUR

5

1

2 BLD. DE L'EMPEREUR P

P

3

6

7

R. DE L'HOPITAL

Plan for the refitting of the site
1-4 Pavements-terraces and the large staircases
2-5 Boulevard de l'Empereur replaced to the level of the site
3-6 Pavements-terraces and the large staircases descending to
the mall of trees towards the base of the city
7 Mall of trees
8 Public library
9 Corner property reconstructed
P New entrances to parking

9 Site plan.   10 Elevation of the facade towards the boulevard and section of the public staircase.

73

11 Proposal.

12 Existing situation.

Project IV
A destroyed corner near the Théâtre Royal de la Monnaie.

The visual impact of this small corner site extends throughout the district of the Théâtre de la Monnaie, one of the rare homogeneous architectural ensembles in the historic centre of the city (1819).

A simple solution, largely inspired by the district's architectural characteristics, can re-establish the balance and beauty of the well preserved streets surrounding the Théâtre de la Monnaie and at the same time revitalise the entire aesthetic perception of the city centre.

The very favourable situation for a new building would be convenient for the installation of stores and apartments of fine quality.

Translated by Christine Murdock

Demetri Porphyrios
POLYTECHNIC OF CENTRAL LONDON
F GREEN, A GROSSMAN, T KARAVIS

1 F Green, perspective view of the Student Union from the river.

In the past few years the Greek Government has shown an unusual interest in the design and planning of Greek cities. Recently, numerous planning studies of many cities were commissioned. In parallel, the newly formed 'Public Company for Housing and Planning' (D.E.P.O.S.) has undertaken a number of urban renewal projects which, having the nature of pilot studies, would investigate possible alternative models for the physical reconstruction of dilapidated urban areas.

It appears, however, that most of the urban models of the 1950s and 60s which – in the experience of Western Europe – have dismally failed, are still highly esteemed among certain 'progressive' circles of Greek architects and planners. Surely this is quite understandable since the destruction of the urban fabric which Western Europe witnessed in the second half of this century did not take place in the cities of Greece – mainly due to difficulties in financing large scale state or corporate urban renewal projects. Instead, the cities of Greece have suffered greatly from an uncontrolled speculation of land and from the lack of any comprehensive masterplan.

In that sense, while the small building contractors were to inhabit the grim world of petty-scale rapaciousness, architects and planners alike have been contemplating that date when their ever-postponed dreams of realising the urban models of the 1950s and '60s would become a reality. Urban renewal models like those of the 'Ville Radieuse', the 'Stem-and-cluster', the 'Estate', etc are still today, in the eyes of many Greek architects and planners, the innocent panaceas of a 'brave new world'.

The critique against Modernist planning which, in the last fifteen years or so, has challenged seriously the foundations of the Charter of Athens has not as yet been fully internalised by the architectural profession. The danger, therefore, of repeating today the grave mistakes of the post-War period is great.

The projects shown here are outline proposals for the organisation of the urban fabric of the district of Kaisariani in Athens which is currently under study. The brief, given as a studio project, was a modified version of the official one – surely for didactic reasons. The students were encouraged to look at the district of Kaisariani as a relatively autonomous quarter based on the urban design sequence of block/street/piazza/neighbourhood. Attention has been paid to the detailed design of selected urban spaces and public buildings not in order to describe definitive stylistic norms (that would be left to the individual designer), but rather in order to give a sense of the quality of scale, mix of activities and space typologies necessary for the reconstruction of the district along the familiar prototypes of the traditional European city.

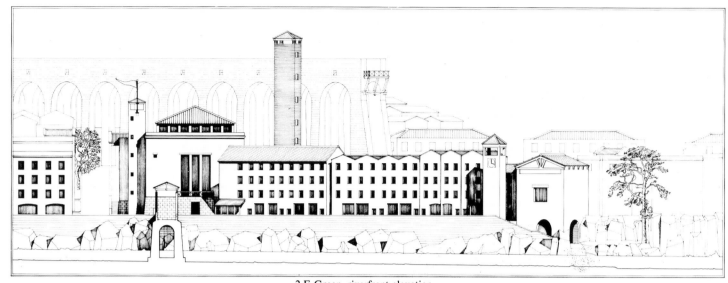

2 F Green, riverfront elevation.

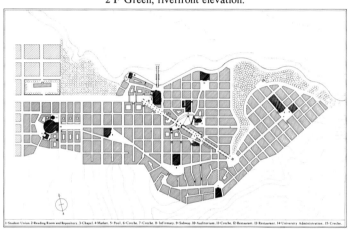

1-Student Union. 2-Reading Room and Repository. 3-Chapel. 4-Market. 5- Pool. 6-Creche. 7-Creche. 8- Infirmary. 9- Subway. 10-Auditorium. 11-Creche. 12-Restaurant. 13-Restaurant. 14-University Administration. 15-Creche.

3 F Green, general site plan.

4 F Green, Chapel Square, general plan.

5 F Green, riverfront and Union Square, general plan.

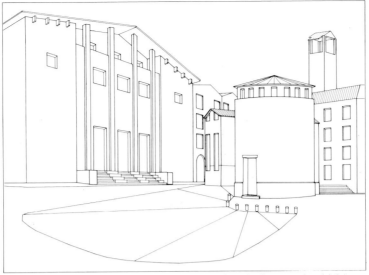

6 A Grossman, perspective view of Theatre (left) and subway station (right).

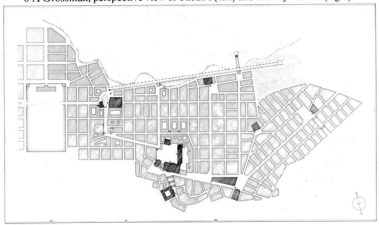

7 A Grossman, general site plan.

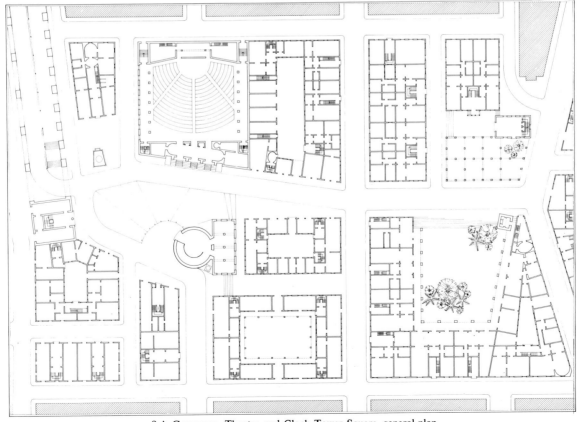

8 A Grossman, Theatre and Clock Tower Square, general plan.

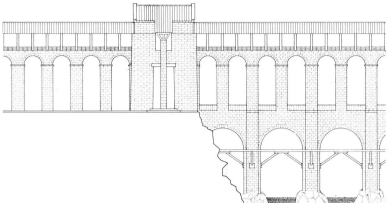

9 A Grossman, Viaduct elevation at Riverbank Square.

10 A Grossman, perspective view of Viaduct entrance from Riverbank Square.

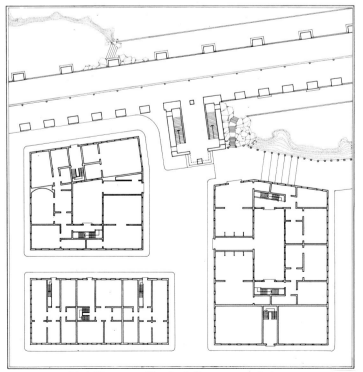

11 A Grossman, Riverbank Square, general plan.

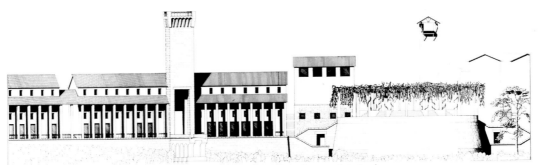

12 T Karavis, riverfront elevation, partial view.

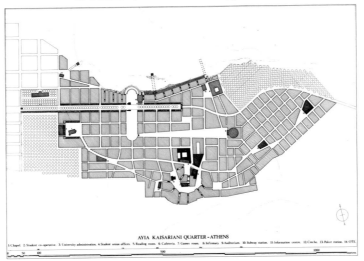

AYIA KAISARIANI QUARTER - ATHENS

1.Chapel. 2. Student co-operative. 3. University administration. 4.Student union offices. 5.Reading room. 6.Cafeteria. 7.Games room. 8.Infirmary. 9.Auditorium. 10.Subway station. 11.Information centre. 12.Creche. 13.Police station. 14.OTE.

13 T Karavis, general site plan.

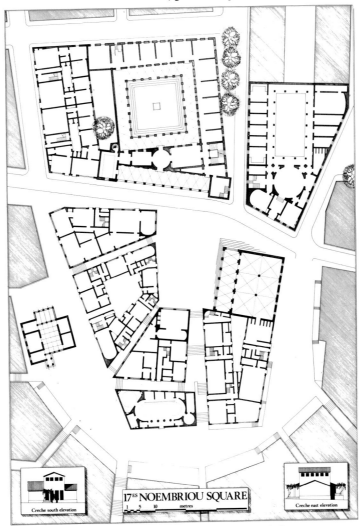

Creche south elevation

17ᴱˢ NOEMBRIOU SQUARE

Creche east elevation

14 T Karavis, Student Union Square, general plan.

Rob Krier
BREITENFURTERSTRASSE, VIENNA

The narrow stretch of property along abandoned brooks, sections cut off from the imposing plan of the aqueduct by the Southern Water Administration, shows no differentiated structure from street and plaza. A look back at traditional Viennese courtyard construction of the 1920s and 30s shows that there once was such a dwelling-complex situated in the immediate vicinity.

In the crowning piece of the triangular house plan east of the aqueduct are a kindergarten and a pedestrian subway leading underneath the road. A round tower, flanked by ramps, shapes the bend of the entire composition. The oval multipurpose room of the kindergarten accommodates the space between the side transepts leading towards the aqueduct.

The round house with its diameter of 32 metres forms the link between the courtyard and the street curvature. The ground floor zone is furnished with arcades toward the inner courtyard where business shops and community

1 Existing aqueduct.

2 Model.

rooms are located. Here, clear accommodation for the entire district must take place. For small theatre performances and concerts a stage scaffolding can be formed. A fountain with a monumental figure group decorates the plaza. The portals, rendering the entrance to the plaza, are differently shaped. An octagonal building and an attenuated structure form the closing of the site.

The outline sketches are fundamentally polygonal; this allows the living rooms to be orientated east-west and north-south. The secondary rooms and hygienic compartments are sympathetically placed away from the noisy street.

With this building proposal I have contributed ten sculptures which are significant components of the applied architecture. I would like to exhibit these works at sculpture lectures, so that architecture and sculpture – working together – may once again resonate.

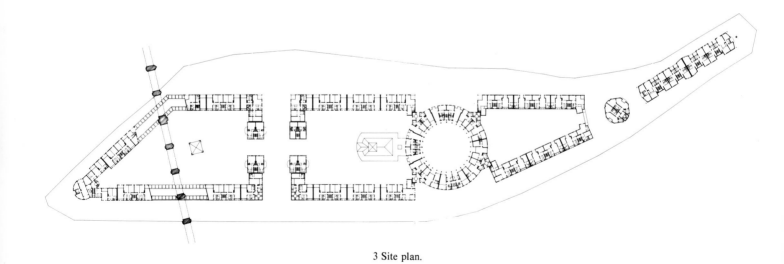

3 Site plan.

4 Sections.

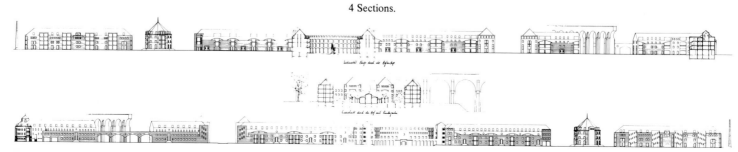

5-8 Perspectives, plans, sections and elevations.

Rob Krier

BREITENFURT CENTRE

Here in Breitenfurt is a shapeless fragmented settlement modelled after an American suburb which I reckon as a kind of antique *agora* (market place) made to order. There, moroever, is the property left over from competitions, still false, and I use this theme in student work without any reference to town planning. They can learn these abilities themselves.

On the site there was not one existing church. This gave me the idea to embellish a covered recreation hall with a tower-like structure, at least to create a sign for the building's administrative and cultural function. In the region there are outstanding stone quarries, from which material the building should be produced.

The half-circular building body of the small town hall easily fits into a U-form. The stairwell with its generous airspace becomes a bright illuminated well by means of a glass roof. Over this well are the accessible town hall assembly

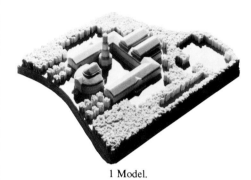

1 Model.

rooms. The well relates to the interior courtyard, building up the structure and stressing its monumentality.

The plinths between the town hall and school pass through two different portals, making the approach to the interior courtyard accessible. Elementary and upper school are built as two-storeyed side transepts; through a lower gallery the tower assembly room and the multi purpose room are entered. The corridors are unusually generous, following the models and plans of monastic cloisters. These also serve in bad weather as recreation halls and as foyers for cultural events. The building's continuous architecture should offer the village a future assembly place for both political and religious purposes. Here, monuments and remembrances of the site's history can be accommodated.

Translated from the German by Christine Murdock

2,3 Plans, elevations and sections of the Town Hall.

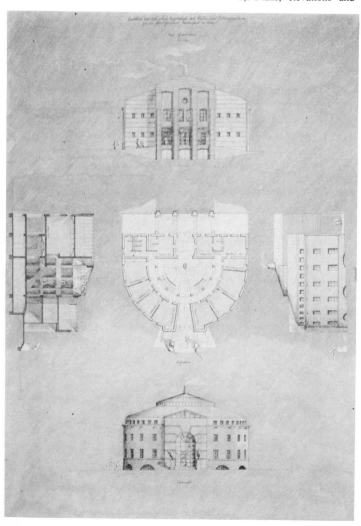

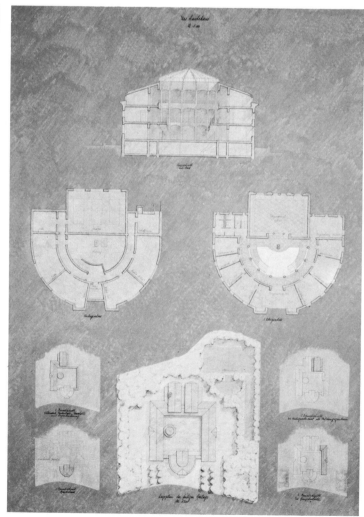

4-7 Perspectives.

Bruno Minardi
CALATAFIMI: THE SPA TOWN

with: *Massimiliano Casavecchia and Franco Castagnetti*
Collaborators: P. Campana, R. Cattaneo, R. Cristofano, A. Cupani, D. Amara, P. Piro, P. Profita

PREMISE

These two projects were elaborated during a workshop at the International Convention on Parks held 1st - 15th September 1980 in Gibellina, Sicily.

The theme of the Convention, promoted by the municipality of Belice (the Sicilian province which had suffered a serious earthquake several years before) was the clarification of several interventionist hypotheses for those small regions where zones lay still dormant and unused, deprived of any valid urban use.

After the damage caused by the earthquake, it was planned that about 1,000 of the 6,000 inhabitants of Calatafimi would be transferred to a nearly level area lying south-east of the existing built-up zone. But for a number of years now, the extensive street layout equipped with sewers, public lighting and footpaths, constructed as part of an unbuilt residential estate (planned by ISES but never realised), has been lying there unused and devoid of homes.

One of the themes proposed at the Convention on Belice was to redesign this area, giving it an urban appearance: something which didn't happen from the casual hypotheses and elaborate fragmentations of ISES. This project was devised, more or less, from the existing street layout. The recent discovery of a spring offered an opportunity to present this little town as a true spa.

To tell the truth, I preferred not to attend this workshop because I wasn't interested in developing or planning a city: I prefer the study of smaller elements and leaving the rest to chance rather than predicting so many things in one improbable bull's-eye . . .

My project is based on some elementary observations which may have, in part, opened a few hypotheses at the Convention:
1 The complete confirmation of the existing

1 Existing situation.

street layout: this not only for a sound criterion of building economy but also because in my opinion no beautiful or ugly streets exist if their design doesn't unify or contribute to the value of the surrounding buildings: the Crescent in Bath, separated from the long edifice it accompanies, would only be a curving street.
2 The confirmation of a connecting outer city road axis: as in unplanned market towns as opposed to foundation cities, the making of a commercial bridge-head on a heavily trafficked route represents in fact the most coherent development possible.
3 The choice of an orographical or mountainous element as an organisational feature. Lacking pre-existing or new buildings, the intervention goes a long way towards healing the pomposity of a long wall of estate housing cutting the horizontal curves of a gradient overlooking the urban development. By constructing the Great Tower on this slight hill and

by making the same wall of estate housing become a long grand building that follows the line of the terrain, the geography becomes, as in antiquity, the architecture.

Organised by these references, the project itself articulates a general hypothesis of road conditions and traffic, and is an indication of other residential typologies while arranging other emergent forms.

The arterial road connects the spa to the north with the old Calatafimi and to the south with the tollbooth of the motorway entrance. Onto it there faces a long continuous series of structures for hotels, restaurants, amusement arcades, shops, an open-air cinema: these buildings compose a long built-up thoroughfare, marked during the day by a lofty row of date-palms and at night enlivened by the forest of multi-coloured neon signs.

The grill-restaurant spans this great entrance avenue to the town (like the 'Pavesi' grill-rooms on the motorways), forming a huge coloured gateway.

At the side of the avenue a vast parking place shelters arriving cars so that the entire internal part of the city centre is for pedestrians: those who wish may take advantage of small overhead cable cars that leave from the parking area to the Tower.

The spa is a large complex building visible from every part of the town. It also houses the urban administrative services, school, kindergarten and possibly other collective facilities.

Between the avenue and the spa, set at an angle of 45° to the former, is the housing for people living and working in the town: terraced and detached homes which follow the lines laid down for the endangered districts which were built immediately after the earthquake for the population of the Belice valley; in these, I in fact found a spontaneity and sociability not easily found in definitively reconstructed areas. It is certain that whoever visits Belice today could consider the sequence of shanty towns that have become deeply rooted around the old centres as elements of landscape that have more vigour and vitality than new 'rationalised' villages.

Translated from the Italian by Christine Murdock

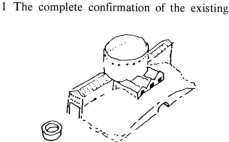

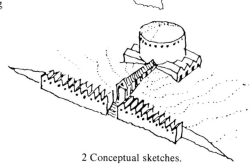

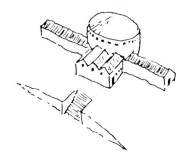

2 Conceptual sketches.

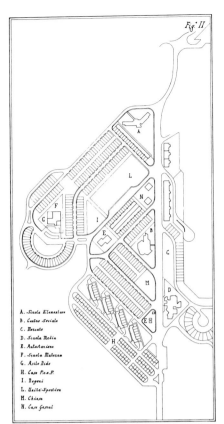

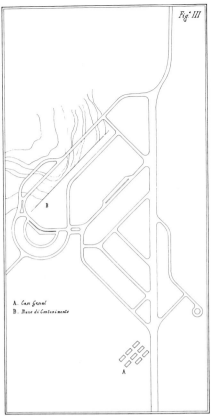

Fig.ª II

A. Scuola Elementare
B. Centro Sociale
C. Mercato
D. Scuola Media
E. Autostazione
F. Scuola Materna
G. Asilo Nido
H. Case P.e.e.P.
I. Negozi
L. Unità Sportiva
M. Chiesa
N. Case Gescal

Fig.ª III

A. Case Gescal
B. Muro di Contenimento

Fig.ª IV

A. Albergo
B. Strutture Ricettive
C. Negozi
D. Cinema Arena
E. Torre Orologio
F. Funicolare
G. Parcheggio
H. Grill Ristorante
I. Case a Schiera
L. Villini
M. Terme

3 Site plans.
4 Axonometric of design proposal.

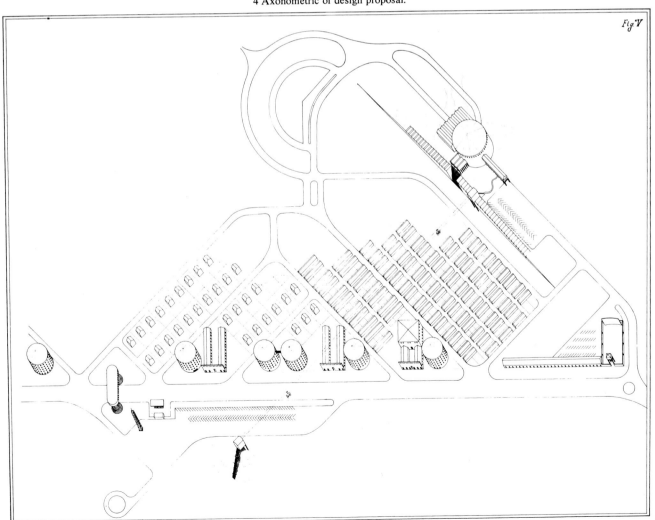

Fig.ª V

Bruno Minardi

MAZARA DEL VALLO: THE CANAL PORT

Bruno Minardi with M. Casavecchia,
F. Castagnetti, D. Amara, B. Campana,
R. Cristodaro, A. Cupani, D. Piro, R. Profita

Mazara, an ancient town going back to the pre-Greek period, a Phoenician port, Roman castrum, Byzantine town, was occupied by the Arabs in 827. The town, which stands near the ancient Selinunte, then became the focal point of the whole valley. At present Mazara is the largest fishing town in Italy.

This project takes up the recent development of the canal-port of Mazara del Vallo, which envisages an early transfer of deep-sea fishing boats to the sea dock, freeing the section of the river that traverses the town for possible tourist use.

The plan proceeds in part by isolated elements and, in part, by built spaces within which repetitive and repeatable building sections can be inserted. The decisive part in this dialogue with the location is played by the constructional material, above all the vague suggestion of dock machinery that hangs over the most prominent buildings, such as the bridge (whose span has a compass-opening to permit the passage of sailing boats), the bar-restaurant made entirely of enamelled metal, and the lighthouse trellis.

Features of the project:
1. Large metal trellis lighthouse sited at the entrance to the river to mark the transition from harbour to sea. The lighthouse is placed symmetrically in relation to the statue of S Vitus, the

1 Existing situation.

2 Conceptual sketches.

patron saint of the town.
2. Footbridge on the location of the old ferry which used to link the two banks of the river, joining the two waterfronts of the town and creating a great 'gateway' over the river. In line with the tradition of drawbridges, this structure is a cross between a building and a machine, a dual character emphasised by the differentiated use of materials: blocks of tufa for the bases, which house public toilets in the sub-staircases; enamelled wooden planks for the two entrance cabins of the ramps, which house the machinery for opening the bridge; enamelled sheet metal for the roofing and enamelled iron for the piers resting on the river bed; iron again for the footbridge, which opens as two equal sections by means of a compass-mechanism.
3. A small dock, made out of a pre-existing drydock, to be used for sheltering pleasure craft; around this little harbour, a screen of buildings made of tufa contains the services for the tourist port on the ground floor and dwellings on the upper floor; this built up space on the waterside will be enclosed like a small shipyard.
4. The bar-restaurant Al Porto, built on a pier in the dock and jutting over the water, is the focal point around which the whole project is designed.
5. An iron and canvas shelter is placed on the small square in front of the dock: it covers the local fish market, which brings back to the town a part of the fishing activity that is so important for the inhabitants.

3 Site plan.

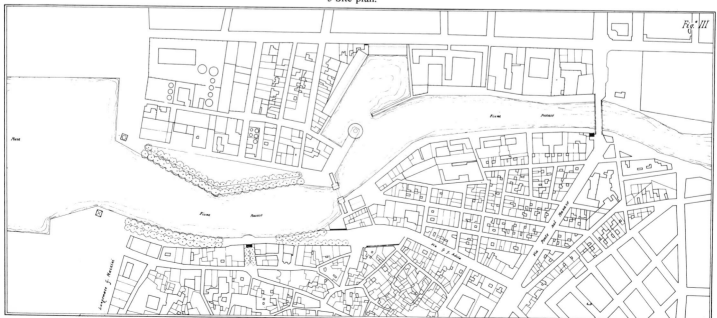

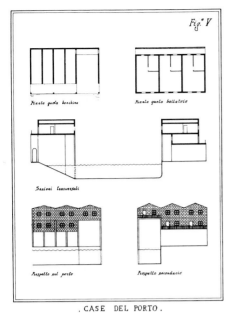

Fig.ª V

Pianta quota banchina   Pianta quota ballatoio

Sezioni trasversali

Prospetto sul porto   Prospetto secondario

. CASE DEL PORTO .

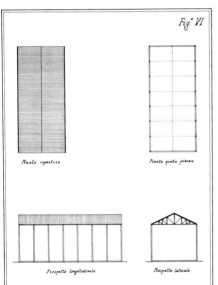

Fig.ª VI

Pianta copertura   Pianta quota piana

Prospetto longitudinale   Prospetto laterale

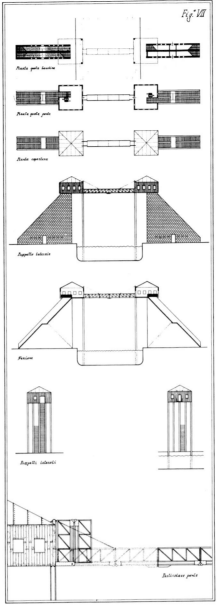

Fig.ª VII

Pianta quota banchina

Pianta quota ponte

Pianta copertura

Prospetto laterale

Sezione

Prospetti laterali

Particolare ponte

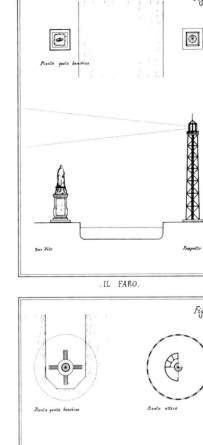

Fig.ª VIII

Pianta quota banchina

San Vito   Prospetto

. IL FARO .

Fig.ª IX

Pianta quota banchina   Pianta attico

Prospetto   Sezione

4 Plans, elevations and sections.

5 The new dock.

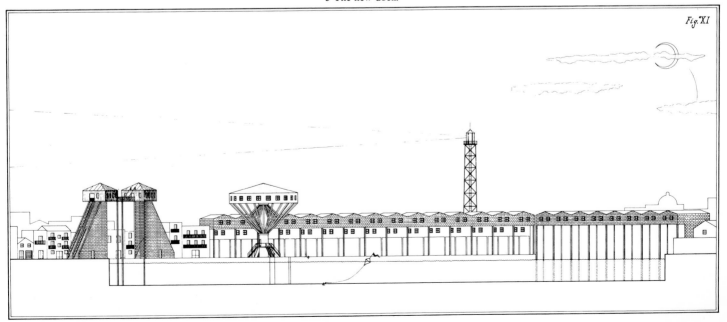

Fig.ª XI

87

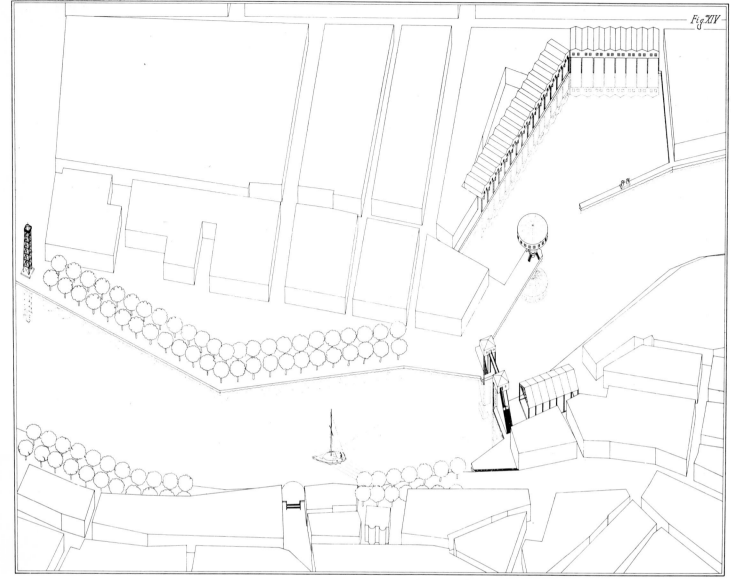

Fig.XIV

6 Axonometric.